The Composition Instructor's Survival Guide

BROCK DETHIER

Foreword by Donald M. Murray

Boynton/Cook Publishers
HEINEMANN
Portsmouth, NH

Boynton/Cook Publishers, Inc.
A subsidiary of Reed Elsevier Inc.
361 Hanover Street
Portsmouth, NH 03801–3912
www.boyntoncook.com

Offices and agents throughout the world

The author and publisher wish to thank those who have generously given permission to reprint borrowed material:

"Adjunct" first appeared in *Composition Studies,* Spring 1997 and "Genesis" in *The Exchange* 5, 1997. Reprinted by permission.

"Ballad of the Girl Whose Name Is Mud" from *Collected Poems* by Langston Hughes. Copyright © 1994 by the Estate of Langston Hughes. Reprinted by permission of Alfred A. Knopf, Inc.

Library of Congress Cataloging-in-Publication Data
Dethier, Brock.
    The composition instructor's survival guide / Brock Dethier :
foreword by Donald Murray.
       p. cm.
    Includes bibliographical references and index.
    ISBN 0-86709-489-3 (acid-free paper)
    1. English language—Rhetoric—Study and teaching.   I. Title.
PE1404.D39 1999
808'.042'07—dc21
                                     99-15380
                                       CIP

Editor: William Varner
Production: Vicki Kasabian
Cover design: Jenny Jensen Greenleaf
Author photo: Donna Horchner
Manufacturing: Louise Richardson

Printed in the United States of America on acid-free paper
03 02 01 00 99   DA   1 2 3 4 5

To the University of New Hampshire composition staff 1979–1997,
who through it all had fun

Contents

Adjunct

With a Bartleby of Arts
and a doctorate in Denial,
I've survived four Chairs,
three Deans and
six or eight Directors.
Student butts beyond count
have squirmed in my one chair.
My floor is white with dead letters.
My recycling box is always full.

Take the stairs to the top—
no Penthouse here—
hang lefts until you see the end.
Where the hallway dies, that's me—
King of the Dead End,
Master of Intermission,
Sultan of Sour Grapes.

The ceiling is low,
the walls very high,
there's a window into a shaft.
The perfboard's covered
with crayoned monsters,
tales of freak beheadings,
the shelves are filled with
books thrown out by those who rose.

Read the screed
outside my door,
genuflect before you knock—
in a year if you're lucky
you'll be on the tenure ladder
at the College of Great Benefits
while I'm teaching your replacement
how to climb.

Brock Dethier

Foreword

Donald M. Murray

This book should be in the backpack of everyone who teaches Freshman English, basic or advanced composition, or who supervises the staff who teach these courses. It is a survival manual—and much more. It is also a significant book of composition philosophy, pedagogy, composition theory, and practice. *The Composition Instructor's Survival Guide* achieves a pragmatic idealism that will help each instructor prepare for class and conference as well as respond to student drafts.

As creator and supervisor of an advanced composition program, as Director of Freshman English, as English Department Chairperson, I knew that most of the best teachers of composition were the least paid. Few receive health benefits, fewer still are included in retirement plans, and almost none are given a living wage. These academic mercenaries may teach part-time or full-time, and most teach more than "full-time" professors. They include graduate students, many of whom had extensive teaching experience before they arrived on campus; many are faculty spouses; they may even have advanced degrees and publications yet they are the English department's invisible faculty.

Still, I found they were often the idealists of the department, dedicated to teaching, their subjects, and their students. They could reach a broad range of students, teaching both those whom others thought unteachable and even those more difficult students who think themselves able to write and are beyond instruction. The invisible faculty instructs the young and the old, English speaking and non-English speaking, prepared and unprepared, motivated and resistant, overconfident and terrified, balanced and unbalanced. And an amazing number of students learn. They learn grammar, usage, spelling, rhetoric—and much more. They begin to think critically, to organize what they think, to make it clear to the instructor and their classmates, to discover and hear their own voices and the voices of others, to listen and to read—critically and with delight. They learn to value their lives and, even more important, to value their individual responses to their lives. Brock Dethier has been a member of the invisible faculty at three universities—he is one of the best teachers of composition I know. When I was his supervisor, I discovered a demanding but caring teacher. I often sent him the most difficult students. And teach them he did.

I became, in a very real way, one of his students, and thanks to all the devices of this age—fax and phone, snail mail and e-mail—I am his student today. He is the single best line-by-line colleague I have. He asks tough questions of my drafts and me, reads my revisions and listens to my responses, makes suggestions that I—almost always—accept. This wise, practical book will stand on the shelf near my computer. I recommend *The Composition Instructor's Guide* to anyone who is teaching writing or learning to write.

Acknowledgments

This book is one long acknowledgment to my writing students and colleagues of the past twenty-three years. I have tried to give credit when I could remember to whom I owed it, but a complete acknowledgment would list the thousands of people who have passed through my classrooms and my offices. I will note only those whose names still come to me easily and beg forgiveness from those who were more generous to me than my memory is to them: Rick Agran, Eqbal Al-Rahmani, Pam Barksdale, Tim Barretto, Derrick Brewer, Ken Brewer, Heather Buckels, Steve Buzzell, Paul Cadigan, Tom Carnicelli, Tracy Chafe, Elizabeth Chiseri-Strater, Mary Clark, Ruth Clogston, Desiree Crane, Hildred Crill, Tim Dansdill, Anne Downey, Ed Drouin, Erin Eborn, Mark Edson, Will Evans, Les Fisher, Kathryn Fitzgerald, Alice Fogel, Joe Freda, Cinthia Gannett, Keith Grant-Davie, Don Graves, Barry Greer, Karen Harris, Jan Harrow, Lauren Howard, Christine Hult, Hilse Jacobsen, Lysa James, Peter Johnson, Dot Kasik, Carol Keyes, Ji-Soo Kim, Tessa Kunz, Tom Lacey, Barry Lane, Jack Lannamann, David Levin, Shelly Lieber, Gary Lindberg, Stefan Low, Andrea Luna, Lisa MacFarlane, Dianne McAnaney, Mekeel McBride, Sheila McNamee, Chris McVay, Lynn Meeks, Bob Merrill, Andy Merton, Joyce Vining Morgan, Tamara Niedzolkowski, Tom Newkirk, Andrya Packer, Margo Page, Tony Pallesci, Mary Peterson, Laura Provan, Donna Qualley, Dan Reagan, David Robinson, Ann Ronald, Shanan Roos, Rebecca Rule, John Sandman, Kent Saxton, Janet Schofield, Julie Schum, Ed Sears, Leaf Seligman, Carrie Sherman, Sarah Sherman, Margaret Shirley, Kevin Shumaker, Warut Siwasariyanon, Kathryn Sky-Peck, Leslie Stevens, Bill Strong, Virginia Stuart, Patricia Sullivan, Jeannie Thomas, Barbara Tindall, Phil Wade, Chris Walsh, Dave Watt, Judy Wells, Sue Wheeler, Ann Williams, Bronwyn Williams, Sheila Wilson, Jill Wolski.

Bruce Ballenger's comments on a draft of this book both improved the book itself and gave me a new model of successful friendly critiquing. Our conversations about writing over the past two decades have consistently shaped and inspired my own work.

A casual question from Ralph Fletcher provoked the final chapter.

My debt to Don Murray is incalculable. His thinking infuses every page of this book. His support has made it happen. Although I never took a class from Don, for twenty years he has been my chief mentor, guide, inspiration, teacher, job agent, and source of knowledge about everything from WWII firearms to raising grandparents. He is the best writer and the wisest person I know. Writing teachers who don't know his work should come in out of the cold. When he first invited me out to lunch, knowing only that I was a faculty spouse interested in writing, he told me he'd be the one in the faculty center foyer who looked like Santa Claus. He was right, and his bag of gifts still seems bottomless.

Everyone thanks a spouse but few can claim an in-house editor to equal my wife, Melody Graulich, editor of *Western American Literature,* elegant writer, and superb teacher. Her belief is often my only fuel.

Bill Varner of Boynton/Cook has provided the right suggestion at the right moment throughout the process of creating this book.

My parents modeled for me the attitudes I advocate in this book: my father, Charles Dethier, taught English with more joy than pay for thirty years; my mother, Maisie Dethier, is a master of making the best of imperfect circumstances.

Prologue
Happiness Is the Best Revenge

With nothing but an innate knowledge of grammar for a guide because the teaching comp class won't be offered until the following semester, the petrified graduate instructor stands before a roomful of students for the first time, Strunk and White clutched desperately in one hand, knowing they're all thinking FRAUD.

Trying to recall the attractions of this profession, the freeway flier heads for the day's third job: four classes at the voc-tech in the morning, conferences with the first-year students at the University in the afternoon, now a continuing education fiction writing class that runs until 9 P.M., unless, of course, no one shows up, as happened last week when it snowed.

After two years of teaching composition, the part-time instructor has a bag full of good tricks but worries about the lack of shape, direction, or continuity to the semester, about pulling tricks out of the bag randomly like cards from a deck.

Reading the alumni bulletin, the master instructor becomes deeply depressed, the occasional gratitude of students and admiration of colleagues paling beside the world-valued successes of classmates and the University's refusal to pay as much for a decade of composition expertise as it does to hire a new janitor.

This book confronts the dilemmas faced by these and other teachers of composition: How can we respect ourselves and what we do in the face of scorn even from our English department colleagues? How can we keep our eyes focused on the intrinsic rewards of our jobs when the tangible benefits elude us? How can we appreciate the advantages of being invisible yet struggle for recognition? How can we be selfish and reduce the time, the stress, and the responsibility of our jobs but still provide students with one of their best college experiences? How can we rise above the daily traumas of the job to remember that it's fun?

I will argue that no matter how unfair our pay and unflattering our status, we can triumph over the system only if we enjoy what we do, rejecting the academic focus on esoteric publication and classroom aloofness, choosing instead the joys of working closely with other human beings to develop the skill that defines us as humans. Happiness is the best revenge.

But it's elusive. Most of the thousands of people who teach college composition in America are not on a tenure track and have little hope of becoming professors. They are, in the words of one instructor interviewed by M. Elizabeth Wallace, "not the low men and women on the totem pole. We are the part deep underground, holding the whole thing up" (16). Though they're often treated badly by their institutions and departments, their love of teaching their subject—and/or their sense of having no options—keeps them at it, sometimes for an entire career, often fighting burnout and feelings of inadequacy and underappreciation.

I know. I've been teaching college composition for more than twenty years, never in a tenure-track position, never making a salary commensurate with my education, experience, or ability. I've been all those people sketched at the beginning of this introduction and have taken on dozens of other teaching roles. At times my lowly status and all the prejudices that go with it loom large in my consciousness. Like many composition instructors, I am often angry or depressed about my job.

But this book is not a litany of injustices done to teachers of composition. Anyone who has taught composition for a year or two doesn't need to be reminded of the job's drawbacks. (And anyone new to the subject should get a copy of Barry Greer's collection, *Paper Graders: Notes from the Academic Underclass*, a powerful multigenre indictment of "academic slave labor" [37] and the "exploitation, manipulation, and double-talk" [70] so common in the treatment of instructors.) I accept the unfairness of the composition world as a starting point and try to answer the more difficult question: How can we make things better? What can composition teachers do today to get through the next student conference or the next stack of papers with more pleasure, more confidence, more sense of accomplishment?

This book advocates cultivating an attitude that finds value in the hectic, overworked lives of composition teachers. I do not want to be misconstrued as saying that this value is enough, that we should stop agitating for better wages, better status, better working conditions. We need to do all we can to change the way the institution views us and our discipline, but we also need ways to stay enthusiastic and fend off bitterness while those glacial processes take place.

For readers consumed by despair, anger, and the suffocating feeling of living below a very low glass ceiling, I'm afraid I can't offer a step-by-step method that will yield on-the-job happiness. Fully enjoying and appreciating what we do would require discarding entirely our culture's notions of "success" and "career." Many institutions still insist that composition teaching should be a temporary step for people on the way to something better. The job certainly isn't for everyone; it's more taxing for most graduate instructors than teaching literature would be, and many people who have completed their degrees simply can't afford to teach full-time for half-time wages, no matter how many intrinsic benefits the job offers.

I can't *persuade* someone to see the benefits of invisibility, to trade dreams of corner offices for the realities of occasionally grateful students, but it's possible to inspire. As Susan McLeod attests, enthusiasm is catching (119). I taught in one department where teaching assistants boasted about how many students had cried in their offices, and no one, it seemed, could stand to teach composition; they were just doing time until they could graduate to esoteric seminars on their favorite literature. At the University of New Hampshire, by contrast, we traded stories of teaching breakthroughs, student insights, and new ideas for tomorrow. Even people quitting to go elsewhere and make real money would say with regret, "I love my job. I wish I could afford to stay."

I've been thinking about these issues since the early 1980s, when I wrote "First Time Up?," a guide to the UNH composition program intended to make new graduate instructors feel less overwhelmed by their jobs and more confident in their own abilities. Writing that guide helped convince me that celebrating the personal rewards of teaching composition provides instructors' best hope for combatting despair and burnout. We need to see and value how much teaching teaches us. We need to have faith in our discipline and consciously build respect for ourselves and the work we do. We need to learn how to reduce the often exhausting amount of time we spend on our classes without shortchanging students or losing the crucial sense that our work matters.

This book begins by describing long-range, broad, often intangible goals that composition instructors can work towards, such as building respect and learning to appreciate the intrinsic benefits of the job. It moves to more specific, practical, immediate suggestions about dealing with common sources of instructors' headaches and creating a great class even when all plans go awry.

My definition of "composition instructor" is, of necessity, inclusive and somewhat vague. According to *Market Data Retrieval,* nearly forty thousand people teach college composition and writing in the United States. A small percentage of them are full-time, tenure-track professors; the rest I'm calling "instructors." It is a heterogeneous group—some have doctorates, some have master's degrees, some have just a bachelor's and a hurried orientation. Some teach one course per year, others ten or twelve. Some aspire to tenure-track positions, some just do their jobs, others want only to teach. A few people I've talked to have tenure but because of their continuing struggle for recognition and appreciation for themselves and their discipline they identify themselves more with nontenured instructors than with tenured composition rhetoricians, theorists, and administrators. Linking all these disparate people are an enthusiasm for teaching and a sense of being underappreciated by their institutions and by the public.

I can't make them pay us better. But after twenty-three years of studying the composition profession through my own eyes and those of hundreds of colleagues, I've grown adept at seeing and articulating the rewards of this profession, the things that keep us—despite all the drawbacks—reapplying, competing for the chance to earn high-school-grad wages teaching three sections per semester without benefits. I think I can explain the inexplicable: why so many people love this job.

1

Build Respect

"I learned to write because Mrs. Moulds had high standards. Wouldn't let me get away with a thing. Your papers for her were perfect, or you had to copy them all over again."

"Those people who teach Freshman English spend all their time getting the kids to express themselves, and they come out of there not having a clue what a formal report is."

"Every year test scores go down, and yet they'll tell you that diagramming sentences doesn't work."

"I don't see why we shouldn't get rid of Freshman English. Those students couldn't write worse than they do now."

"English was always my worst subject. Seems like all English teachers do is tell you what's wrong with you."

"Anyone who writes can teach writing. There's no content to it."

From the guy driving the airport shuttle to your father-in-law, most people are awed by writers and have a sense of inferiority about their own writing. But though they're probably not up on process methodology or research about the effectiveness of formal grammar instruction, many have strong beliefs about how writing should be taught, what aspects of

English should be emphasized. And they're likely to have a low opinion of the work we've been doing.

Some such feelings are justified—many people have had writing experiences that would make anyone bitter and resentful. When the chemistry teacher assigns a five-hundred-word essay on water to the lab partners who enacted a squirt-bottle High Noon, the punishment may seem rehabilitative and educational—certainly better than filling the blackboard with "I will not squirt my classmates." Yet either assignment teaches "writing is punishment." Many courses also require writing only during essay exams, with the course grade riding on the outcome, time running out, brain cramps and dry pens afflicting the unfortunate. Some of the same people who use writing as a punishment or a test pass the buck about writing improvement, blaming others for a problem they may have exacerbated themselves. So writing teachers often wind up feeling the scorn or anger of both the punisher and the punished.

Building respect for writing and writing teachers is a seemingly endless process made particularly difficult because so many social forces stand in the way. (Educators of any subject share some of this difficulty; as Clabaugh and Rozycki point out, much of the current national debate about education may be based on "Machiavellian intentions" (398) of politicians who want to keep teachers' salaries low or limit the definitions of education.) Building respect requires action at every level of public life. For most of us, that means trying to enlighten people around us, exposing and articulating damaging attitudes whenever we can, not letting prejudiced ideas slip by unnoticed.

Changing public perceptions of writing and writing teachers may well be hopeless, especially given the number of people who simplify their lives by blaming us or who thoughtlessly make the act of writing more difficult or more painful. But the Sisyphean task is worth undertaking because as we articulate the reasons that our jobs and our discipline deserve more respect, we build our own self-respect and increase the clarity with which we see our own value.

Build Respect *In the Public Sphere*

Few people question the expertise of the physics professor or the pedagogy of the math teacher. Yet millions of Americans and the school boards they vote for feel they have a right to say what should be taught in English classes and how it should be presented. We're not just talking about the easily dismissed local crank, either. Even the National Collegiate Athletic Association gets involved in writing training by judging which high school English courses to accept as part of an athlete's "core requirements," upon which the athlete's college sports eligibility rests. Grammar and "vocabulary development" head the list of what the N.C.A.A. likes to see in an English class, and a number of athletes have lost a year of eligibility while fighting to get credit for nontraditional high school English classes. Critics charge that the N.C.A.A. often judges classes on name alone and savored the irony when the *New York Times* printed (using *sic* three times) a sloppily written rejection letter sent out by the N.C.A.A.'s Initial-Eligibility clearinghouse (Applebome).

The tenacity with which people insist that students should be taught "spelling" and "grammar" (and should find it just as odious as their parents did) makes me think that the battles about English expertise concern more than just writing. Perhaps people sense that education in general isn't the way it used to be or should be—that information, pedagogy, and the world in general have become too complex and alien—and they focus their criticism on English as the most familiar and approachable discipline. Perhaps the millions of dollars publishers would lose if English teachers abandoned workbooks and grammar texts have something to do with it too.

In any case, asserting our expertise is not an easy matter, especially because whenever we identify ourselves as writing teachers, we get assaulted with "Ooops, better watch my grammar." I have a hunch that few of the people who demand a return to sentence diagramming would really want to *listen* to an explanation of why that's not a great idea. But when we do get a listening audience, it's important to be ready.

1. Let people vent. Most people have a reason to be antagonistic towards writing and writing teachers, and if we let them rant about it, chances are we'll be able to agree with them that it was mean of their sixth-grade teacher to read their essay as a bad example. We can trade tales of our own embarrassment and assure them that we try to be supportive and that our methods are, if not new, at least, as Wendy Bishop says, "retheorized" (139). It's hard to get too mad at the dentist who says he too hates to be drilled.

Most anger is a response to misinformation—people think we don't believe in punctuation or polished writing. We can gain support by letting people know that we believe in high standards and grammar; maybe we should tell people we've vowed to never let a split infinitive go unmarked.

2. Open our ears. We may value the expressive over the vocational aspects of our courses, but the public's insistence on mechanics masks a plea for practicality that we can't ignore. I've had students whose progressive, process-oriented English teachers told them throughout high school, "We'll worry about the superficial stuff later." When they get to me, the last writing teacher before they hit the job market, they're desperate for someone to correct their comma splices. Composition teachers should be the last academics on earth to engage in ivory-tower thinking, yet when we get immersed in a subject that interests us—whether process methodology, poetry, or social constructivism—we need to start asking whether we're teaching for the students' benefit or our own.

3. Acknowledge that writing IS a "craft and sullen art" never completely perfected. We have to inform the public (including many of our university colleagues) about the complexity of writing and teaching writing. Many people think writing is typing and writing training is teaching spelling ditties. We need to let them know about the time we spend on research and revision, attitude and procrastination, organization and order, logic flaws and outlines. They might feel less adversarial towards us if we explained that our teaching, and the discipline in general, is constantly evolving. We don't yet know how to do everything right, but we're confident that some hated methods of the past don't work—bleeding red ink corrections all over the page, teaching grammar in isolation, focusing solely on error.

4. Clarify the relationship between writing and thought. Essential to a proper sense of respect for writing is the understanding that writing is thinking, necessary for almost all of us to create, expand, develop, organize, connect ideas. I keep a copy of Marvin Swift's *Harvard Business Review* article, "Clear Writing Means Clear Thinking Means . . . ," to give to people who think that writing is essentially stenography, taking down in functional code what had already been thought through. Swift shows how a businessman who sets out to polish a trivial memo clarifies his thinking as he tightens his prose and ends up completely changing the policy he was writing about.

5. Insist that good writing is everyone's responsibility. Parents, siblings, peers, teachers of all subjects at all levels influence a child's language development. Blaming—or crediting—a particular English teacher for a student's writing ability is akin to holding a football coach responsible for a runner's speed. We also know that a student's writing can vary radically from one paper to the next, depending on the student's motivation, knowledge, procrastination, interest in the subject, and scores of other factors. We've seen papers that our ex-students have written for other classes and been appalled at how good writers can revert to semiliteracy. The performance on a particular paper depends on the assignment and the assigner; if the professor—or boss or parent—provides an enervating assignment and doesn't emphasize good writing, students won't put in the extra effort to move from "getting some ideas on paper" to writing an excellent analysis. We can't do our jobs alone, a fact that should provide the impetus for a variety of extracurricular writing programs.

At the same time, not everyone who writes can be a successful writing teacher; people not in our profession need to *learn* how to play a role in writing improvement. Starting with a sense of humility in the face of the subject's complexity, they can move on to such basics as the value of revision and feedback and of emphasizing and grading aspects of content and writing that really matter, not just those (like spelling) that are easy to spot.

6. Know the research results: Results show that teaching "grammar" in isolation has no positive effects. That children know the essential grammar of their language before they enter school. That we usually learn from whole to part, through discovery and development of our own hypotheses. That only certain kids will ever understand English grammar (though others may well become good writers). That many writing "errors" are a sign of experimentation and a necessary component of writing growth. That we learn reading and writing best by — surprise — reading and writing. Constance Weaver's *Teaching Grammar in Context* is a first-rate resource for quickly getting up to speed on what we know: it provides both summaries and in-depth analyses of the most important research on teaching grammar and writing.

7. Talk money. People who cheer when education budgets get slashed should know that small class size, one-on-one contact, and energetic teachers propel writing improvement, and they cost money. No one expects to train biologists without fancy labs, cutting-edge computers, and well-trained teaching assistants. Yet perhaps because you can write with charcoal on concrete, the public expects writing training to be next-to-free.

8. Expose the grammar cops. Unfortunately, the public is less likely to hear our reasoning than to read the columns of language "mavens" like William Safire, James J. Kilpatrick, and the late Edwin Newman, who put the worst possible face on writing improvement. I applaud their interest in language and the excitement about etymology that they sometimes profess. But the ominous sense of right and wrong that hangs over their discussions, their castigation of those whose usage doesn't match theirs, and their holier-than-thou attitude remind readers of that ultimate English-class horror, the Mr. or Ms. Gradgrind who hoarded writing knowledge to wield over unfortunate students. Though I argue below that we should be slow to criticize other English teachers, I think we should expose the grammar cops whenever possible. That they have an audience demonstrates public concern about writing; I wish such concern would translate into more money for public education rather than for building podiums for the mavens.

I feel the same way about people like Richard Lederer, who makes his living laughing at foolish writing mistakes. Of course some of his collected faux pas are funny, and I suppose his books will be useful documents for future linguists studying attitudes towards language evolution in the twentieth century. But think of the message that Lederer's works communicate to students: "We're watching your every move, ready to pounce and laugh. Be careful what you write! To be safe from our snickers, don't write at all!"

9. Support our colleagues. While distancing ourselves from those who feed off public anxiety about writing, we need to build respect for our jobs by practicing solidarity with our colleagues at all levels. Confronted with complaints about (or, worse, direct evidence of) the sorry state of student writing in their own classes, many composition teachers resort to passing the buck, blaming previous teachers, previous classes. I too jump on the condemnation bandwagon when I hear stories about teachers who were demeaning ("It's spelled right, so I knew you didn't write it") or absurdly rigid. (One high school teacher marked points off for any paragraph that did not include precisely eleven sentences. I'm not making this up; I saw the evidence.) But I try to bite my tongue before I make sweeping judgments about the teachers who preceded me. I remind myself about the innumerable responsibilities of K–12 teachers, most of them involving students who are not college-bound; about class sizes, the impossibility of their jobs, distracting pressures from parents and principals, the validity of different priorities, teen hormones, students' tendency to forget or to remember exactly wrong, television, assaults on the act of writing itself by people who should know better. Janet Emig tells of an evaluating adminstrator who, having stopped to observe a language arts class in which everyone was quietly writing, reassured the teacher, "I'll come back when you're teaching" (135).

Build Respect *In the Institution*

The attitudes of the nonacademic public towards writing are easier for me to understand and excuse than those of many in academia who benefit from the work of composition teachers yet express nothing but contempt for the work those teachers do. This scorn may be composed of many elements: a desire to scapegoat someone for students' writing problems and to relieve themselves of any responsibility to work on those problems; the assumption that because some fledgling graduate students teach composition, all writing teachers are equally inexperienced; the need to cling to the markers of status and look down on those who don't have a Ph.D. or whose salaries don't match their age. Like other professionals from doctors to plumbers, some professors feel comforted by having a wide moat between themselves and anyone else who does similar work.

Unfortunately, attitudes within the English department often aren't much better. Literature professors who've never tried it assume that teaching composition is easy—*"You don't even have to read anything!"*—and that anyone who can write well can teach writing. When some English departments run out of their own graduate students to staff their Freshman English courses, they hire graduate students from other departments, in the most extreme cases giving the job to anyone who "can walk a straight line at 10 o'clock in the morning," as a University of Illinois English professor put it (Wilson, A12). So much for the value of our education and experience!

Administrators face cognitive dissonance and/or budget difficulties if they admit to themselves how badly they're treating the large and talented group of composition teachers. Even tenured professors in composition sometimes want to distance themselves from the rabble who teach freshmen. One of my former bosses assured a faculty group that "anyone can teach Freshman Comp"; another told a national conference that he wasn't going to worry about professional development of composition instructors at his school because he knew that all they wanted to do was take their paychecks and go home.

What can be done about such attitudes, especially those expressed by people who have every reason to know better? I'm tempted to say "nothing," because few things are so immutable as the minds of academics who have decided to hold on to particular opinions to protect their egos.

Hope may come from some who study and advocate educational change. Ernest L. Boyer's 1990 Carnegie Foundation report, *Scholarship Reconsidered,* documents that most faculty decry the "shift toward research, away from teaching" (29) that contributes to the low regard accorded to composition instructors and other student-oriented teachers. Boyer recommends redefining scholarship, adding to the traditional category of research (which he calls "scholarship of discovery") the scholarships of integration, application, and teaching (16–25). If universities were to accept the importance of these three varieties of scholarship, at which most composition instructors already excel, we might find ourselves among academe's most respected scholars. In fact, in the follow-up to Boyer's influential report, Glassick, Huber, and Maeroff found that "the definition of scholarship is being broadened" in 78 percent of all postsecondary institutions (15). If their definition of the qualities of a scholar—integrity, perseverance, and courage (61–67)—achieves equally widespread acceptance, institutions may begin to value their large pool of composition scholars.

But even if such redefinitions seem like pipe dreams and producing long-term change in departments and colleges seems like a losing cause, we must demand respect and a voice about a number of issues. Most involve how the institution treats writing classes, particularly Freshman English.

At many universities, first-year English is the only course required of all undergraduates. While such a requirement might seem to imply that composition is a valuable, in fact essential course in its own right, many faculty members draw just the opposite conclusion: that Freshman English is a service course, in a category with typing or computer literacy classes, and that its instructors should respond to the needs of faculty who teach "content" courses.

A number of points need to be made about this issue whenever "content" faculty are listening. First, composition instructors who set out to serve the faculty face an impossible job. Professors in a particular discipline might concur that students should learn "the case study" or "the formal report" or "a professional style," but would they agree what those things mean? In my experience, even two professors in the same subdiscipline—organizational behavior, for instance—often value radically different qualities in student papers.

Many faculty also haven't looked into the issue closely enough to know what they want students to learn about writing. The complaints we hear most often are about surface issues like spelling and mechanics, yet I assume that if they confronted the question of what should take top priority in students' writing, many faculty would agree that focus and coherence are more important than the "correct" footnote form.

And before content professors throw too many stones at composition teachers, they need to accept their own measure of responsibility for student writing. Bad writing often reflects bad assignments. Vague questions yield vague responses. Even clear, specific questions about issues that don't interest students provoke meandering bullshit. Much of the worst writing I've seen in college came not from eighteen-year-old Freshman English students still trying to find their dorm rooms, but from upperclass students responding to assignments clearly intended to get them to regurgitate the ideas of Milton Friedman and the terminology of John Keynes. So my question for professors complaining about their students' writing would be a double one: What have you done to make it better? What might you have done to provoke it?

Until non-composition faculty become much more aware of writing pedagogy and their own effect on student writing, therefore, they have no business telling composition teachers what to teach or how. Students frequently draw on disciplines like psychology, sociology, and history to write English papers, yet I've never heard of English professors saying to those other departments, "It would suit our needs better if you would emphasize this content and these methods." Professional courtesy and common sense dictate that at most, other professors should suggest goals for a required writing course and leave the how and most of the what to people who know their subject.

Seeing writing classes as service courses unfairly narrows and diminishes their immense value. Writing courses at all levels offer unique opportunities for personal exploration, skill expansion, and professional growth. First-year Writing is "the single most important course in our state colleges and universities" (Wallace, 16) because it generally provides

- the first, the best, the most personal, and often the longest-lasting link between the individual student and a representative of the institution;
- the best opportunity for students to grow and mature through writing about what's important to them, exchanging serious and personal ideas with peers and a teacher, reading and struggling to understand others' attempts to make sense of the world;
- the place where students establish study habits and develop an outlook on academic work;
- students' introduction to the library, research, and academic writing;
- a chance for students to reevaluate and often improve their opinion of their own basic skills in reading and writing;
- a personal connection with the impersonal institution, without which even more students would drop out or flunk out their first year (which almost half of them do at some schools);
- a chance to work through potentially destructive feelings about themselves and their families, and a channel through which they can get help;
- the best possible recruiting ground for English majors (which at UNH has helped make English the most popular major on campus);
- the best opportunity they'll have until senior seminars to participate in small-class discussions and learn the art of oral give-and-take;
- in Kurt Spellmeyer's words, "the last opportunity most students will ever have to discover the relationship of mutual implication . . . between the self and the cultural heritage within which selfhood has meaning" (269);
- a chance to learn that the whole enterprise of college academics can be fun, relevant, stimulating.

We should be proud that composition teachers *do* take the time, *do* respect their students, *do* work with student papers even about graduation and friends' car crashes, *do* put teaching before research. Such priorities should be another source of respect from tenure-line colleagues, but instead they may help explain why many professors are comfortable keeping composition instructors and their accomplishments in the institutional basement—they don't like to have their own more self-oriented priorities put in such sharp contrast.

Ironically, those professors who abdicate responsibility for their students' writing give up their best possible method of helping their students learn their subjects and improve their thinking about them. As E. M. Forster said, "How do I know what I think until I see what I say?" Connecting, organizing, evaluating, focusing, and ordering ideas, finding examples of generalizations and generalizations to fit examples—in fact, all the processes of writing a paper help students learn about the subject in ways that exams can't duplicate. Except in disciplines that deal solely with numbers, teachers haven't done their job—that is, they haven't helped students learn as much as possible about their subject—until they've not only assigned a paper about the subject but worked with students to revise the paper, to sharpen their thinking, to push past their initial easy conclusions, to find new connections and examples, to move beyond "I'm a teenage gambling addict" to see that the addiction is as American as Wall Street. But, not surprisingly, many professors who are quick to denigrate writing classes are also quick to assert that they couldn't possibly spare the time to do this kind of work with students.

If pondering the assumptions about the "service course" generates anger in the reader who teaches composition, that's not a bad thing. Instructors who have made it through the initial period when the frantic pace and newness elbow aside all other thoughts often settle into one of three attitudes—gratitude and complacency at having a job of any kind (a phase usually of limited duration), depression and frustration resulting from a dawning comprehension of how undervalued they are and how limited their prospects are (a depression that often shows they're internalizing the institution's attitude toward them), or anger. I vacillate among these states, but the healthiest composition instructors I know retain that edge of anger. It reflects their self-respect and their refusal to diminish their own sense of their value to reflect their institution's view. It provides the energy to argue for better treatment and, in meetings with professors, to make the kinds of points I've listed above.

Antagonism between composition instructors and university administrators and faculty is not, of course, either necessary or unavoidable, although the facts that create it—the huge disparity between the treatment of composition instructors and of tenure-track faculty—may seem immutable. The budgets of many colleges rely on the cheap labor of "part-time" faculty; according to John Hickman, "institutions can save 60 to 75 percent on faculty costs" by staffing with adjuncts instead of professors (15). But administrators and professors can—and often do—bridge that gap with simple empathy and respect.

When discussing salary and (lack of) benefits with administrators, I feel a bit better just seeing that the administrator is uneasy, embarrassed to be offering so little. Simple empathic appreciation for our jobs and our expertise goes a long way. Through the din of "Why can't my students write better?" we need to hear voices of authority say, "Student A told me he finally learned what good writing was in your class; Professor B said he was impressed with how well his students could negotiate their way around the library; Parent C called me to share her amazement at how much the papers her daughter brings home have improved over the year. I don't know what we'd do without you." The management literature of the past twenty years suggests scores of ways to empower and appreciate workers without paying them more: officially welcome them and introduce them to other faculty, involve them in decisions, acknowledge their expertise, fight to get them longer contracts and more benefits and smaller classes, recognize their achievements in enough detail to communicate the message, "We *do* pay attention to your work, and we *do* care." Judith Gappa and David Leslie discuss forty-three "recommended practices" that, in their words, "promote better performance and more satisfied part-time faculty who are integral members of the faculty as a whole" (215).

Writing across the curriculum (WAC) programs offer significant hope for increasing the respect for composition instructors throughout the institution. The general education writing requirements that often accompany WAC programs force students and faculty to think more about the place of writing in the non-English course. Often just the campus-wide debate about such requirements can give composition instructors a voice they've never had and raise the general consciousness about writing. When UNH was considering changes in the general education writing requirements, composition instructors volunteered to attend all of the meetings. Deans and professors who might never have been inside the English department witnessed that "those people who teach Freshman English" were articulate and knowledgeable.

With new requirements on the books, professors who take their responsibilities for writing seriously attend WAC workshops and may carry ideas back to their colleagues. Motivated by gen. ed. requirements to have students write more in their classes, some professors discover that asking students to write throughout a semester revolutionizes their courses and makes their students seem suddenly smarter. Some learn in workshops that by asking students to use their writing to think through issues, professors can meet part of the writing requirement without having to collect or read anything. Others find the prospect of reading so many student papers so odious that they ignore the requirement. But even that reaction should have the benefit of giving the professor more appreciation for those of us who spend hours every week reading student papers. And anyone who takes the requirement a bit more seriously will gain insight into some of my points listed earlier, better appreciating the relationship between writing and thinking, and understanding that teaching writing involves so much more than correcting grammar.

At present, the WAC tide seems to be moving some writing training out of English and into other departments. It remains to be seen whether most departments develop their own in-house writing experts, hire English department instructors to do their writing work for them, send their students back to the English department for training, or actually train their professors to be part-time writing teachers. All of these options provide potential jobs for composition instructors, either teaching students or training teachers. I'm betting that the allure of WAC programs will fade once administrators realize that programs involving the work of professors throughout the university cost more to achieve the same results than traditional writing classes taught by low-paid English instructors.

As some of us move outside the safe walls of the English department, we shouldn't fear our ignorance of the writing in other disciplines; most of what we know about good writing in one discipline easily transfers to another, and we can learn the special features of a new discipline very quickly. We need to develop our self-respect so we have enough confidence in what we do to be able to walk into a business school or an engineering class and help the teachers and the students write. I felt like the worst kind of impostor when I jumped from Freshman English and Prose Writing to Advanced Business Communication, but the M.B.A. candidates I taught felt lucky to be in the class, and soon I was a respected business writing authority. I didn't have special abilities, nor was I conning anyone; I just examined purposes, audiences, and conventions as I would for any writing task and learned as I taught. And, having immersed myself in bulleting and white space and executive summaries, I became a better composition teacher.

Build Respect *In the Classroom*

Most students can tell at least a couple of horror stories about previous English classes, and many of those stories involve lack of respect: students or teachers making fun of their spelling or teasing them about personal details revealed in a paper or convincing them that they would never produce any decent writing. Creating an atmosphere of respect in the writing classroom isn't as easy as giving a blessing: "I respect you all. Now be happy and confident in your writing." But we teachers do influence classroom respect, even if we don't control it, and after struggling for institutional validation, we feel relieved to walk into the classroom and know that just by doing our jobs, we build respect for our discipline.

I'd like to say we could simply resolve to respect ourselves, our methods, our writing, and our students—their ideas, their writing, their opinions. But respect must be honest and sincere, and sometimes a student's comment isn't serious enough to deserve a serious response, or a paper doesn't show enough effort to warrant praise of any sort.

At such times, I think the respectful approach is tempered honesty: "You can do a lot better than you did in this draft." To let it go, to pretend to see good in a truly tawdry draft, is condescending to the writer. Better to challenge the weakness of the moment than imply that such a challenge would be pointless, that banality is all the writer can ever hope for.

It's difficult for some teachers, especially veterans, to treat younger students as adults because some of them *are* so young, and their behavior seems so childlike. For that reason, I think it's worth resisting the temptation to call any college students "kids" even if none can legally drink. If we think of students as "kids," they're going to fulfill our expectations.

To me, respecting my students as adults means trying to eliminate artificial barriers between us:

- Instead of impressing my students with gems mined from the teacher's guide, I share the book and its insights whenever I use it.

- I believe my students' stories, their excuses for missed classes and deadlines. I'm sure I've been fooled; the semester-end grandparent mortality rate can't be that high. But I'd rather be tricked than make students think I don't trust them. Such trust seldom costs me anything except a little unwarranted sympathy, but it buys me students who are more willing to open up. Sometimes they even work harder to prove that laziness had nothing to do with their earlier shortcomings.

- I tell them when something is bullshit or busywork or when I don't agree with a stance taken by another professor. I admit that I, too, see problems with requiring students to hand in a thesis statement weeks before the paper. When I send them into the library, I try to be honest about the missing volumes and torn-out articles, preparing them for frustration.

- I try to avoid what I consider to be artificial means of building respect: the serious suits and serious shoes, the insistence on "Mister" and "Mizz" and "Professor," the prohibitions against hat wearing and gum chewing, the stiff back that students never see sweat. Such measures often work: they were used by most of the people we looked up to. Everyone respects tweed and wingtips. Unfortunately, dressing casually may distance composition instructors from some of our tenured colleagues who take seriously only people in similar professorial uniforms. In *Teaching and Performing,* Colorado State University Professor Janice Moore, "always Dr. Moore with undergraduates," tells interviewer William Timpson, "my authority equals my expertise,"

insisting, "Male teachers should wear a sport coat and tie or a vest—
something 'non-student'" (xiv-xv). I realize age, race, and gender
complicate this issue, and as a balding white male, I have it easy. But
I'd rather impress students—and professors—with who I am and
what I know. I don't want to think that I'm getting across to students
when in fact they're just in awe of my shoes.

One of the great joys of teaching composition is the freedom to be yourself in class. People who are pretty much the same inside the class and out are,
I think, the most likely to survive, to feel they haven't sacrificed so much for
the job.

Sometimes when respect takes the most effort or seems most unearned, giving it pays off most handsomely. I usually do in-class writing assignments on
the board, and while I think that act in itself is important, I have to be careful
about how I present my writing. It seems natural to dump on the garbage that
I put on the board—compared to what I *can* do, it often *is* pretty bad, after
all. And my habitual defense against criticism is the preemptive strike—if I
bomb it first, other critics won't feel that they need to.

But succumbing to that self-critical reflex is damaging on a number of
levels. First, my board writing is probably of roughly the same quality as my
students' notebook freewriting, so if I seem to be criticizing my own, I'm im-
plicitly criticizing their work, bringing that nasty critical editor into the picture and undermining the whole point of freewriting. To the extent that my
writing sometimes outshines theirs, they could see my self-criticism as being
disingenuous and hypocritical, fishing for compliments when I should be
supporting them.

Much better, I think, is to show? develop? fake? enthusiasm for whatever
I've produced, to celebrate the process, its successes and the garbage necessary
to yield those successes, to respect all of my own ideas and writing, even if I
discard most of it. We need to show that we can at times turn off the critical
editor, what Gail Godwin calls "The Watcher at the Gate," and just be creative,
something that we may encourage our students to do but that they seldom see
demonstrated.

Respecting students goes beyond treating them as individual, adult
human beings with ideas worth reading and listening to. As people like Tom
Romano remind us, all student reactions to texts deserve respect, because all
are based on their own logic, their own reasons, even though such logic may
seem to us blatantly faulty (1995, 163).

We must also respect their lives, their excuses, their priorities. A student
who misses a deadline because she went home to her grandmother's funeral

is, I think, displaying good judgment—the paper can wait. The student who misses a deadline because she danced all night at a Pearl Jam concert might get a little less sympathy from me, but she'd still get my respect—I wish I'd made more such decisions when I was an undergraduate. A writing class is a defining part of some students' college careers, but for others, it will never be more than a requirement. We have to respect their decision to sacrifice good work in our required course in order to do their best in their major courses . . . or to pursue the relationship that may be their top priority for the moment. Students gain respect for us and sometimes actually put more into our courses when we acknowledge that they have their own valid way of seeing English as less than crucial. We have to respect ourselves enough not to debase our discipline by coercing or cajoling students to get interested in writing or punishing those who don't make it job number one.

Build Respect *In Ourselves*

Instructors tend to be a self-effacing group. Like Judy Wells' Part-Time Teacher, we have egos that are "understaffed" (2). We devote a lot of energy to supporting others, finding the good in marginally literate papers, emotionally holding hands with a whole class full of students trying to work through their hangups about writing. We see the enormity of the task, the students who don't improve, our own inadequacy in one of the many skill areas we have to be good at, and conclude "I don't know what I'm doing. I'm a fraud."

Every writing teacher I know has felt that at some point. I won't pretend that I can affect that core attitude or that taking to heart every suggestion in this book would necessarily make teachers feel they really know what they're doing.

How we present our self-doubt to our students is, however, another issue. I'm a firm believer in admitting our own shortcomings once in a while. I regularly tell students who ask arcane citation questions "I'll have to look it up" (or "*you'll* have to look it up"). I'm with Romano in thinking that we don't show students often enough how we make meaning from initial confusion when reading (1995, 164). In general I believe one of the most important things I can model for students is the ability to admit mistakes or ignorance. One of the women interviewed by Mary Belenky and her colleagues tells the story of the best day in her English class, when students brought up ideas the professor hadn't considered, and "teacher and students collaborated in constructing a new interpretation" (221).

But there's a big difference between "I don't know that" and "I don't know anything," which some teachers express either because they really feel that way or because they're looking for sympathy from students. That sympathy plea can work—my first class gave me some of the best evaluations of my life, in part, I think, because they saw how much I needed affirmation. But young grad students and instructors sometimes struggle because their students see the teacher's admitted weakness as a breach in the wall of authority through which they eagerly rush.

We need to respect ourselves and what we do and know. Teachers must convey confidence. Though we may come out of grad school or job searches seeing ourselves as losers, we can become believers by acting as though we believe in ourselves, playing the role of "teacher who really knows what she's doing," and gaining strength from students' unquestioning acceptance of our scholarly ability and credentials. We need to treat some of our own work as professional writing, worthy of the respect and attention of the class, and we can do that best by helping each other. After a colleague invited me to her class as "guest fiction writer" to read a story recently published by a local literary magazine, I figured, "If it's good enough for her class, it's good enough for mine." Students are almost always interested in my "serious" writing; many clamor for more.

At the end of my Teaching Writing course, I leave students pondering a different kind of self-respect: respect for our instincts. I present them with one final paradox: as they grow as teachers, they need to be humble so they can learn from their students, their experiences, their colleagues, and new thinking and research; but they also should be confident that they have what it takes to teach writing. If they can avoid reverting thoughtlessly to traditional approaches—"the way it was done when I was in school"—four years of training, a lifetime of writing experience, and a good heart will carry them through their first experiences at the blackboard. Good instincts can't overcome a lack of education, an ignorance of research, or serious personal writing weaknesses; and unlike many people who come out of graduate English departments, I see a lot of value in courses that focus on pedagogy, not just subject areas. But I think caring and all the abilities that that word connotes—being sensitive to others and their needs, wanting both to help others and to encourage their independence—determines, more than any other single factor, how good a teacher is. In Nel Noddings' terms, "As teacher, I am, first, one-caring" (176). Freire calls such a teacher "a partner of the students in his relations with them" (62).

So the most important thing we must respect is our instincts. We don't have to know all the theory (although it doesn't hurt). We don't need Ph.D.s or endowed chairs or six-figure salaries to do great work. For both the students' sake and our own, we need to be as much ourselves as possible in the classroom. That means making decisions about student problems as teachers *and* as human beings. And it means building a level of optimism about our teaching. How many people get to be themselves at work, guided by creativity and experience, and to watch other people transform in response to their character and talents? I'm sure I'm not the only composition instructor who has made more money and gotten more credit at other jobs yet come back to teaching writing because I like the me who teaches.

2

Recognize What We Get From Our Jobs

We Learn

In a paper on Tim O'Brien's The Things They Carried, *junior English major Heather Buckels argued that the book's structure—fragments building to a whole—is so effective because, as she'd learned in public speaking, we have abysmal attention spans: we stay focused for only about three minutes at a time. If you speak for an hour, you'll risk snores unless you break your message into twenty segments.*

As I read the paper, I suddenly understood a major trend in American culture: why three-minute rock songs have driven twenty-five-minute symphonies from the airwaves, why hip current books like Generation X *are sprinkled with thought-bites, why Kurt Vonnegut has always been contemporary, why Postmodernists have so much to talk about. The market rules, and the market wants products you don't even have to chew to swallow.*

I now think of "the Buckels principle" as I shorten my paragraphs, insert headings, boil my letters of outrage down to three sentences, explain to students the value of white space. I see the world through a student's eyes.

To survive as writing teachers, we have to see, appreciate, value, glorify what we get from teaching. It often takes an act of will to ignore the paycheck and the three-legged office desk and concentrate on the wisdom nineteen-year-olds have to offer. But veteran teachers manage to do just that. We *all* learn from students, whether or not we label it learning. I borrow most of my stories from students; I learn most of my lessons through their papers.

The gains from such learning are inexpensive, readily available, and varied. To harvest them, we need only the right attitude, some combination of humility, curiosity, desire to learn, and respect for the students themselves.

So what have I learned from students? What it's like to race motorcycles on ice, to raise a horse, to suffer through a bipolar episode, to be disowned by your father, to be a teenage gambling addict. Without clearance from my HMO, I have experienced scoliosis, alcoholism, Crohn's Disease, Turner's, Lou Gehrig's, Alzheimer's. I've survived deadly car crashes, lived on a submarine where everyone smokes the same cigarette, pierced my tongue.

Every day, one of my students holds up a little mirror in which I can see myself. I get a sense of what I must have been like as an undergraduate by observing John over a semester—he works as hard as he parties, trying to determine his allegiances, discovering various subtleties and joys of writing. Watching Sheila juggle kids, jobs, and classes, I gain a new appreciation for single parenthood. Seeing the light in Emily's eyes when she talks about the song "Dry," I know I should listen to P. J. Harvey's music.

As less student-appreciative colleagues keep reminding me, our students —at least most of mine—ARE young. They do foolish things, some of them in class. They write junk fairly often. But that doesn't have the effect on me that it has on some people, provoking the conclusion, "I'll take you seriously in five years." I see in the nineteen-year-old the same intelligent, energetic person who may appear more obviously in graduate school. Some of that future person may be just emerging, and I like a front-row seat to watch the cocoon crumble.

We learn *about teaching our subject*

Most English teachers must labor to forget their own successful infatuation with English and to imagine what less proficient writers feel when they try to use a semicolon. Most of us have an instinct for grammar, including fashionable punctuation habits. But how can we articulate that instinct so that our students who weren't born with grammar ears can learn not to fear the end of a clause? My students seem to base their punctuation decisions on a mix of ear and poorly remembered "rules" from the past. Handing out pages of comma and colon rules never worked for me. I wanted to make simple and consistent those bedeviling dots and dashes.

Eqbal taught me how. She's now an economics professor at Kuwait University, but for six years we struggled together to figure out *the* and other incomprehensible subtleties of the English language. Like many who learned

English in British-influenced schools, Eqbal called periods "full stops." The driving metaphor was what I needed.

I now teach punctuation from the point of view of the reader driving through the prose. What kind of sign does the writer need to provide so that the reader will be best prepared for the road ahead? The options: a comma to say "take a quick breath"; a colon to advise "here comes a restatement"; a semicolon to warn "here comes another independent clause." Parentheses are street signs, dashes billboards. Writers don't need to know the specific rules of punctuation use; they just need to know how readers react to the quite short list of punctuation marks. Let highway engineers debate the regulations.

I can't claim that my students all now use semicolons confidently and conventionally, but many feel better about punctuation, less adversarial towards rules. And I feel less frustrated about punctuation because I'm giving students a sense of the whole as well as the parts.

As we work with and listen to students like Eqbal, we learn. We continuously evolve as teachers in response to our planning, writing, facilitating, conferring, reading, grading, editing. Such evolution makes us into better teachers and, if appreciated, even celebrated, can keep the job endlessly interesting.

We learn *about ourselves*

Teaching writing puts particular pressure on teachers to reveal and understand themselves. It would be hard to avoid some growth in self-awareness as we write about ourselves in front of the class and give students advice about everything from how to remember *effect/affect* to what to do with their lives after graduation.

I learn who I am by examining what I choose to talk about and how I choose to teach. Other people play a variety of roles in that process. A UNH colleague, Leaf Seligman, inadvertently reassured me about my teaching by presenting to the staff an approach to structuring our classes to be consistent with our values. As evidence of her approach, she showed us her syllabus, which reads like a warm letter between friends, with none of the contractlike qualities of my own syllabi. For a few days I worried about what my business-like, multiheaded syllabus said about me and toyed with the idea of presenting myself more the way Leaf does—after all, aren't I as warm, sensitive, and antiauthoritarian as she is? But I realized finally that teachers provide warmth in different ways, and I may be more concerned than Leaf is about making sure that students know the exact limits and requirements of their semester. I know that to reduce writing anxiety—one of my primary goals—I have to make my expectations of my students as clear as possible. So my businesslike syllabus *does* reflect who I am.

Students sometimes write what could be fables from my own life, and I need only keep my eyes open to get a painless lesson in being who I want to be. Donna embodied demure: quick, bright, attentive, yes, but not assertive. In her first draft about her father's breakdown and psychological resurrection during the family crisis meeting in the barn, Donna portrayed herself as an observer. When her father conquered the dragon of self-doubt at the end, the victory seemed like the work of an unseen wizard. Pushed to explain the transformation and her own role, she produced another draft in which she explored not just her father's actions but some of the history behind those actions. Her quick sentences of reassurance to her distraught father, which were hidden away, mumbling, in the first draft, now appeared to be the scene's turning point and the culmination of Donna's long-standing efforts to help her father see more of his own value.

The fleshing out of the characters and the scene not only improved the paper but changed my own thinking about father-child relationships. I learned something from Donna's father that I never learned from my own — the value of admitting weakness, of asking for help. And Donna's successful propping up of her proud father's ego inspires me to offer more potential props to my own father, even if he doesn't ask for them.

Composition teachers get most of our positive reinforcement from watching such papers improve, from cheering such personal insight and growth, from the comments of ex-students heard firsthand or through the grapevine, from talking to colleagues who have "our" students in later classes or to current students who take the time to tell us directly how much they've learned or how their attitude has changed. (Treasure those thank-you notes!)

But we also learn about ourselves from that most feared student assault tool, the class evaluation. As experienced as I am at squeezing value from an apparently thankless job, I can't claim that I always look forward to reading evaluations. Like many teachers, I find it easy to forget the praise, the tales of revelations and transformations, and remember, dwell on, fret about the one or two negative evaluations that show up in almost every class. If the only way to validate teaching was to see what students said on evaluations, composition teachers would be a very glum group, and this book would be very short.

Evaluations can, however, provide unique insight into who we are, as teachers and as human beings. For a long time I assumed that all teachers brought the same kind of energy to the classroom and the same kind of empathy to the student conference as I do, but after reading hundreds of students' comments on those characteristics, some filled with surprise and delight, I finally have to accept that students don't take those qualities for granted, and I shouldn't either. I may consider my colleague Brian smarmy and vacuous, but I can't argue with scores of students whose evaluations show that they're excited about writing because of his class. Evaluations are especially valuable because we can assume that students' comments—particularly the positive ones—are honest, not colored by ulterior motives as are almost all face-to-face comments.

We fear evaluations in part because anyone can read them but no one has a proper sense of context in which to assess them. Much of that fear is justified; I've been amazed at the confidence with which administrators sometimes draw conclusions based on very debatable interpretations. They summarize students' comments on a teacher's warmth as, "She mothers them." A wide variety of positive comments reveals, "There's no coherence to his teaching."

But observing this process of evaluating the evaluations has also taught me important, stress-reducing lessons about reading my own evaluations. Administrators often read with approval certain negative comments—gripes about tough grading; too much work; the teacher being too demanding, expecting too much of students, asking students to rely on themselves too much. Some administrators also worry about too-rosy evaluations: "If everyone's happy, I'm suspicious," one of my former bosses said. So students' saying "bad" may bode well for their teachers.

We also learn from the way we evaluate others. Analyzing the student behaviors that particularly annoy me helps me understand myself and perhaps shrug off some of the annoyance. If I've taken the time to fix a "not only . . . but also" construction on a student draft or to substitute *tenure* for *ten-year,* I don't like seeing the same mistake, uncorrected, in the next draft. I'm irritated, I realize, because the lack of response to my penciled correction seems to show that they weren't paying attention to me . . . that I wasn't having the kind of effect I wanted . . . that I may be wasting a lot of time writing comments . . . that my whole reason for teaching is suspect. (On the other hand, my wife suggests, it may show simply that the students don't see or can't read all of my penciled comments. Red ink used to be the medium of choice for a reason.)

We learn *about our world*

Luckily—for our profession and for this book—writing teachers themselves thrive on the prompts and advice most useful to students. When I give open essay assignments, I require only that the student really care about the subject; it has to matter. To get students thinking about what matters to them, I use a number of prompts during the first few days of a course. Students jot down an authority list of all the things that they know more about than do the other people in the class. Then they create a want-to-know list of questions and issues they'd like to pursue but have never taken time for. I might also ask them to list the traumas in their lives, the turning points, the unresolved conflicts.

The widely varied papers that spring from these kinds of prompts share one similarity—they arise out of the students' knowledge, experience, or expertise, not mine. So rather than wince at their half-baked ideas about Hamlet's motivations or their distorted view of the 1960s (two subjects that I *do* know something about), I can honestly be an innocent and ignorant reader, eager to learn more, asking questions not to lead the writer to a conclusion I've already reached, but to help the writer fill in the gaps in the paper.

Taking such an attitude towards students' writing has obvious benefits for the student, who may feel less manipulated by my questions than does the student writing about "my" subjects. Like anyone else, students enjoy feeling like the experts, and if I don't overwhelm them with questions, they often get excited about answering, explaining, demonstrating what they know.

But for me, this process has benefits similar to those of opening an encyclopedia at random and memorizing the first entry that catches the eye, a technique of those legendary by-the-firelight scholars. After twenty-three years of reading student papers, I know a little about a lot of subjects. Of course the papers of undergraduates tend to cluster around certain topics; I've read more about binge drinking than about the pain of watching a spouse fall apart. But I enjoy getting to know a bit about creating a haunted house, the problems of Vietnam veterans' kids, how twenty-year-olds cope with friends dying from overdoses, social stratification in Mexico. I don't think my friends yet view me as a walking Webster's, but I doubt I'll ever get tired of opening up the next paper, thinking, "What will I learn here?"

We learn *about how others think*

I never understood objections to "swear words"; the term itself sounds archaic and childish. Sure, if you overuse any word, it gets repetitive and boring, and there are some words I would never allow in my classroom (*nigger* is the classic example) because they're so patently demeaning to a particular group of people. But my tendency was to see objections to the bulk of race- and gender-neutral words as irrational prudishness passed down from generation to generation, with no one questioning, "Is this word really hurting someone?" When one of my wife's students wrote on an evaluation that her class was "not for the delicately bred," all we could do was laugh.

But I've developed more sympathy for the "delicately bred" as the result of a discussion about something I *didn't* do last fall. The article for the day in my Research Writing class discussed the effects on listeners of rap and heavy metal music. To provide an example to react to, I decided to play Ice-T's "Cop Killer," perhaps the most controversial song of the 1980s, which, conveniently, uses elements of both musical genres. Listening to it at lunch, I began counting the uses of "the F word" and the "M-F word" (as I later referred to them in class), and I began to worry that my class full of Latter-day Saints would be appalled and outraged.

I carried my boom box to class but never plugged it in, opting instead to describe the song for the class and ask if anyone would have been offended if I had played it. A number of students raised their hands, and one explained her objections in a way that I could relate to: she said the words created images in her mind that she didn't want there; in effect, they polluted her imagination. That idea may seem absurd: no imagination could be as polluted as reality. But I could relate: I go to very few movies and watch very little TV because my own imagination is easily polluted by visual images. Occasionally, despite attempted mental censorship, scenes from the first movie that I wish I'd never seen, *The Devils,* appear unbidden in my mind: wasps stinging plague buboes or the good guy burning slowly at the stake. Words alone don't have a similar effect on me, but I now realize that if I am going to run the risk of creating such durable and unwelcome images in my students' minds, I'd better have a very good reason. I'm more likely now to see a real thought process, a legitimate reaction, where before I saw irrationality and prejudice.

We learn *about what others value*

It's tempting to assume that composition instructors who share the same general goals and many of the same methods also share values and priorities. So it's important to be reminded that some people can't stand one-sentence paragraphs and say toe-maht-toe. I want to understand others' values enough so that I appreciate them and don't thoughtlessly dismiss or denigrate them. In the process, sometimes those values actually sink in and affect my own.

I'm no fan of staff meetings where we all grade the same papers and learn that we don't much agree, but that disagreement reflects some differences worth paying attention to, if only to provoke ourselves to challenge our own assumptions and priorities. During such a session, I learn that Sue will overlook sloppiness if a writer can hold her attention with specifics. Bruce wants to see some surprise or discovery in any paper he considers for an A. Althea can't grade the paper out of context; she would have to know how much the paper had improved since the last draft in order to grade this one.

Mark gives it a high grade because it has a focus and a purpose; Mindy cuts it down because it has so many comma splices and sentence fragments.

I don't ignore any of these factors, but hearing that others make them top priority keeps me more honest as a grader and sometimes helps me see new worth in the papers I read.

We learn *why it matters*

It's easy to get cynical or defeatist about the whole enterprise of teaching composition. Students haven't learned to enjoy writing or to use semicolons in twelve years of English classes, so what chance is there that they'll suddenly change now? Even if they do become lively, personal, detailed writers, their next professor will probably penalize any use of "I" and reward them for vocabulary regurgitation and pervasive nominalization.

In the face of such realities, we need to keep rediscovering why it matters, why this job is worth doing.

It matters because Chris's mother, at the U to pick up her son for summer break, insists that she meet me in person just so she can tell me how pleased she is that in my class Chris wrote about his father and finally expressed some of the anger she worried was dangerously bottled within him.

It matters when Chris himself writes ten years later to say that, although he was a history major, he had followed his writing passion to get a job as a reporter and is doing great.

It matters when Kelsey first admits to herself that she does have strengths as a writer and when Whitney writes on her evaluation that she has learned writing can be fun. It matters when Terri writes a tribute to her dying mother and sends it off in time.

It matters when Robert's summer grant proposal is accepted and when one of Julie's essays gets published.

It matters because students may never get another chance to write about their anoretic sister's death, to work intensely, one-on-one, sentence-by-sentence with an experienced professional, to improve what may be the central skill of their adult life, to think for themselves and have that thought treated with respect.

I'm not sure I've saved any lives, but I do know that my class is sometimes the one academic thread a student clings to. My course doesn't produce millionaires, but it gets people excited enough about writing to become English majors and get writing jobs. My students haven't saved the world, but some of them are working on it, and they first learned to mix passion and information in my class.

It matters.

We Grow

Laurie didn't say anything during the first meeting of my Prose Writing course, and when she stayed after class, I assumed she had a typical first-day question about requirements or schedule. She hung back behind the other after-class students, so we were alone when she said to me, "You're an agent of the devil."

Now, depending on the source, I might take such a remark as a compliment or at least remarkably insightful, but coming from a student who'd seen me for only eighty minutes, it seemed a bit bizarre. The immediate source of her feelings, it turned out, was that in explaining why I had ordered the class books from an alternative bookstore downtown I had dumped on the university bookstore, where she worked. She told me later, by way of apology, that she was also distraught about family problems: she was a born-again Christian, spending all her free time at a local antiabortion clinic, but her equally devout grandmother had rejected her denominational choice, and the clash of theologies was tearing her family apart.

It also absorbed all of Laurie's time. By midterm, she had produced only a few feeble, half-baked drafts, and as I gave her a D+ for her midterm grade, I debated encouraging her to drop out and try again another semester. But I knew she was smart and could write, and I decided to extend her more rope. With a month or so left in the term, Laurie's personal problems cleared up, and she started cranking out one good paper after another, eventually earning a B+ for the course. I considered her the great success story of the semester until I read her evaluation. Her summary of the teacher? "He was too lenient."

When I read Laurie's assessment, I didn't know whether to laugh, cry, or rage through the halls; it definitely left me feeling that I couldn't win. As I discussed in the previous section, student evaluations are explosive documents, difficult for even the most experienced instructors to deal with. But as ironic as it may seem, this particular evaluation not only taught me something, it helped me grow. Though I am still easily hurt and depressed by student comments, I have achieved a modicum of distance and objectivity toward them. As a result of Laurie's line, I now *feel*, rather than just intellectually *know*, that many student comments say much more about the student's life and problems than they do about the teacher being evaluated. Laurie helped me see that I sometimes simply know better than my students. I'm confident that allowing Laurie to rebuild her belief in her own writing was the right thing to do, and though kicking her out of class would have taught its own useful lessons, they would have been humanly and pedagogically inferior.

I hope that most occupations stimulate personal growth, but I doubt many can compare with teaching composition. Because we learn so many of the things I outlined in the first section of this chapter, growth is almost inevitable, and if we pay more attention to our learning and make it more conscious, we grow more.

We grow *through listening to ourselves*

I suggest to Derrick that he try brainstorming more before he sits down to a first draft, I encourage Maryann to consider her letter of reconciliation with her boyfriend the most important writing she's doing, I tell Walter that his pessimistic outlook on his own work undermines his considerable abilities. And all the time I'm thinking, "Maybe I should do a little more prewriting," and "Stop feeling so guilty when you write long family letters," and "Quit shooting yourself in the foot with bad attitude."

After I've said something to enough students to make it part of my repertoire, it's hard for me to ignore its implications in my own life, and I try to be a better writing student, more consistent with my journal, more patient about jumping into the first draft.

Near the beginning of my career, Richard Larson, while he was editor of *CCC*, helped impress upon me the value of learning my own lessons. I had submitted to *CCC* an article called "Using Reading to Teach the Organization of Writing," and Larson, though he liked the piece, encouraged me to use my own method on my own work. Embarrassed, I did, and turned it into a better article. We gain a lot from doing as we say.

That experience encouraged me to look at my own writing as a source of my growth. In retrospect, I realize that I wrote "In Defense of Subjective Grading" in large part to feel less guilty and conflicted about my admittedly subjective grading practices. Thinking that issue through on paper and making it convincing enough that someone would publish it made me much more confident about my own stance on the subject. Similarly, writing this book, culling ideas and attitudes from my decades at the bottom of the academic ladder, has helped me feel more comfortable in my job, less annoyed with the constant insults to my work and my position.

Having realized how much of my writing and advice answers my own questions, how many of the questions I ask students spring from my own doubt, I can both grow more from my own insights and be a better teacher. I now find myself modifying the strength of my advice when I realize that I, not the student, need to listen especially well, and to avoid feeling too hypocritical, I either try to do what I advise, or I stop harping about it.

We grow *through humbling ourselves*

I've met few composition instructors with runaway egos, but anyone who teaches needs frequently to change roles and become again a humble student.

My starting to take poetry seriously in middle age has given a great boost to my teaching and my writing. Although I took some poetry writing classes in college, for the first twenty years after I graduated, I wrote everything but poetry, frightened off by the vague feelings that I wasn't any good at it and that somehow the genre itself was too effete, rarified.

My attitude began changing when I started teaching Critical Analysis, a course that includes a section on poetry. I searched the anthologies for poems that excited me and gradually became a poetry fan. Reading it with pleasure made me want to write it, and I found that being a novice in a different genre helped me identify with the way my students felt sailing unsteadily into uncharted waters. Being able to say honestly "I'm a beginner" is liberating.

Though I'd been preaching "show, don't tell" for years, writing poetry finally taught me what that means, as my poetry group would regularly slice off the final, explanatory lines of my poem. I learned that one of my strengths as a writer is my ability to say "it's good enough for now" and let it go, knowing that I can go back later and make the bumbling prosaic lines tighter, more visual. And my small, naive insights about the genre can have vast implications: I'd always thought traditional poetic forms, meters, and rhymes artificially confined the poet, but experimenting with them shows me they can nudge me out of my thinking ruts, trick me into making connections I might not have made if I hadn't been trying to rhyme *Katahdin*. Recognizing the inventive prod of rhyme, I look again at traditional forms in other areas—my syllabus, this book, my marriage.

As a professional reader of others' papers and at times a professional writer, I tend to get a bit cocky about my proofreading abilities and a tad superior to those who turn in sloppy work. But every now and then one of my own overlooked mistakes will make it into the public eye, and I'll realize that older and wiser usually also means humbler. Cases in point: Before a staff meeting, I ran off a memo to all participants offering to do the dirty work that everyone else had shirked, setting myself up as the "sacrificial lamb." Only somehow it came out "superficial lamb," a *jeux de mot* that the rest of the staff appreciated more than I did. I provoked similar laughter last year when I was writing voice descriptions on the board and confused "subdued" with the rock group Subdudes. And I'm sure I've written things that caused snickers I never heard, as did the conscientious management professor who wrote in the margin of a sloppy paper, "proffreading is important." I think of such examples whenever I find myself mounting my high horse about others' writing frailties.

This kind of humbling can, of course, be crushing. But it also reminds us that no matter how good we may be at our joint crafts of teaching and writing, we are still apprentices. Don Murray has led the way in demonstrating how to be a humble master, always teaching but always learning from students, colleagues, words. One of his favorite quotations sums up why I see the reinforcement of our humility as a good thing: Sculptor Henry Moore says, "The secret of life is to have a task, something you devote your whole life to, something you bring everything to, every minute of the day for your whole life. And the most important thing is—it must be something you cannot possibly do!"

We grow *through identifying our prejudices and blind spots*

The first time I taught Composition for Teachers, I assigned everyone to do a presentation and a paper on an issue in composition. I said that they were free to work alone or in groups on the presentation, but when someone asked whether the issue papers should be individual or collaborative, I immediately said, "individual."

Thinking about it later, I questioned both my answer and the speed with which I delivered it. One of the groups (all men, interestingly) had chosen "collaboration" as their issue, and as we talked about the subject, my reasoning began to look pretty lame. I said at the time that I was concerned with the difficulty of grading a collaborative piece, worrying that some people would coast and some would do extra work they would never get credit for. But as we discussed the benefits of collaborative work, I saw that they outweighed the drawbacks, and I began to realize that the heart of my objection was less than rational. My experience with collaboration hadn't been particularly bad: The one time I had assigned collaborative papers, two groups out of eight had been disasters—people dropping out at the last minute, leaving their groupmates stranded. But the rest of the class thrived. In trying to justify my reaction, I couldn't even fall back on "It never works for me," for while I have seldom performed the "four people in front of a keyboard" act that my class group attempted, most of my professional writing has involved serial collaboration: The Writing Guy turns into readable English the notes or rough drafts of content experts. At the root of my resistance, I fear, was what I now perceive as a stereotypically male privileging of individuality and solo work, preferably done in a freezing garret. This prejudice was worth challenging.

Discovering such bias behind what I thought were rational actions helps me become a better, more objective teacher as well as grow as a person. I question my own reactions, and I keep my ears open. I'd be foolish to claim that I have eliminated all bias from my own thinking, but I can point to specific areas of growth that followed from such realizations. I try to curb the competitive urge that dominated much of my thinking before I started teaching: my band is better than your band, my author is better than your author. As I see it now, one of the goals of life is to embrace, find pleasure in as many things as possible, and I can't do that if I'm putting down D. H. Lawrence or refusing to listen to music made on synthesizers.

We grow *through playing shrink*

Composition teachers' taking on the role of psychiatrist makes some people uneasy, and I'm certainly not ready to start prescribing Prozac or pointing the finger of blame for a student's anorexia. Few composition instructors want to overstep the boundaries of their expertise. Yet the engagement with students about emotional issues is often an important, satisfying, and productive element of the composition course for both student and teacher.

In some ways, therapy in the writing course is purer, less complex, and therefore possibly more useful than in the psychiatrist's office: the teacher focuses not on the student but on the student's paper, what it reveals, how it could be made better. As Donna incessantly reworks the paper about her father's big speech in the barn, trying to find what she's really after in the tangle of ideas about him and about their relationship, I can offer more direct help than could a therapist, because I can work on the concrete—the paper in front of me. I can't tell her what to think about her relationship with her father, but I can tell her what the draft says to me, and I can point out where a missing transition might be an opportunity to dig for the meaning produced by connecting the two ideas. Explaining her role improves the paper and helps her see the scene with new eyes and feel better about her father and the part she played in his transformation. Students frame, connect, establish cause-and-effect, and excavate layers of memory and feelings, not because a counselor tells them that doing so might be therapeutic, but because the paper needs it.

Often we do our best work just sitting in conference while the writer tells us what the paper needs and what he or she plans to do about it. Occasionally I get depressed thinking that a brick wall could do that part of our job, but then I remember that I used to pay seventy-five dollars an hour to talk to such a wall.

Sometimes we can spark an epiphany for a student simply by asking the most obvious questions, pointing out the baldest inconsistencies.

"In the first paragraph, you pose the question *Why are some women attracted to abusive guys?* but you don't ever answer it."

"You express all this anger towards your father, but you never say why you blame him for the divorce."

"You're arguing that people should be allowed to carry concealed weapons, but most of your evidence is about gun control in general."

"What would you want the reader to conclude from all this information about breast cancer?"

While making such points, asking such questions, thinking about such issues, we see with double or triple vision—the student often stands in for us, so as we ponder the student's situation, we ponder our own, often seeing solutions for the student's relatively simplified dilemma (we don't know all the complexities) that we would never see for our own. And as we get older, we see more often from the students' parents' point of view. I won't claim that I've ever cured a student's neuroses or purged my own through talking about a student's, but now that I've thought and revised with a manic depressive, several A.D.D. students, hundreds of children of divorce, and people who have recently lost parents, siblings, and friends for the most tragic and heartbreaking reasons, I know more about the human psyche than do most people.

We grow *through listening to our students*

Ex-student Dave comes by once a month. I'm his moral sounding board. He tells me of the latest extreme position he's taken—creating a movie ad in the student newspaper that angered women, writing a letter to the editor questioning the need for more cultural diversity—and my reaction helps him decide whether to be proud or embarrassed. I hope I'm helping him bend in good directions, but as I listen to him I think more about the extremity and exaggeration of my own opinions, and I resolve to lighten up a bit my own public declamations.

I have lunch with another ex-student, Leslie. She says brightly, as if it were a compliment, that she'd had a revelation recently: I'm no smarter than she is. Of course I joke my way through the moment, but when I think about it later, I am stunned. Our whole relationship has been predicated on my intellectual superiority: I was the professor, the Ph.D., she a lowly social work sophomore. I gave her Bs! Surely if I still have anything to offer her, it is my brainpower, my knowledge of the intellectual world.

But as I think more about her words, my consternation decreases. After all, I *want* students to rely on themselves and remove the pedestals from under professors and writing professionals. I have come to count on Leslie's wisdom and good sense as a friend and confidante, so maybe I should be pleased that she ever thought I was smarter than she. Most important, I realize that even though she considers us intellectual equals, she still wants to be my friend, still wants to have lunch with me. Maybe people want to be my friend for who I am, not what I have to offer them . . . Maybe I don't have to ask myself what someone can get out of a relationship with me . . . Maybe people value me just for me.

That probably shouldn't be a revelation to someone my age, but it was worth more than months of therapy. It affected my self-esteem in a way that no compliment could. And it's the kind of insight, the chance for growth, that could only come from talking with an ex-student.

We start growing the moment we start planning for the next class, and as far as I can tell, our teaching-related growth never has to end.

We Connect

Martin looked like trouble. He was the energy in the high school poetry group I'd been assigned for the day. Loud, boisterous, feeding off the attention of the girls around him, he reminded me of students who have given me nightmares because they're more interested in peer attention—even that provided by a reprimand from the teacher—than in praise. As I began somewhat nervously preparing for the workshop, the conversation around Martin lulled, and more to fill the silence than for some brilliantly conceived pedagogical reason, I pointed to Martin's Walkman and asked, "Whatcha listening to?"

"Ween," he replied, with the tone of someone telling a dirty joke that the teacher will never get.

"Which one?" I asked, glad he'd mentioned a New Jersey cult band that a student had turned me on to the previous year. Martin got excited telling me about their latest album, and soon we were off into a five-minute conversation, not Writing Expert and Peon Student, but two music lovers discussing a relatively new and decidedly unusual musical act.

We connect *with students*

Connection is at the heart of teaching writing. We head off many potential disciplinary problems, motivational problems, attendance problems because we have connected with students. When they add some element of "friend" or "peer" to the mixture of feelings about us, students don't see us so much as adversary, agent of the institution to be challenged or attacked, and the benefits spread to every aspect of the class. What Belenky et al. say about women applies, I think, to almost all students: "confirmation and community are prerequisites rather than consequences of development" (194). From the teacher's side, connection makes possible the learning and growth I've detailed so far, and in fact most of the human benefits discussed in this book.

Teaching writing brings us into close human contact with hundreds of people a year, and the nature of that contact is often more honest, more real, than that between any other pair of non-friends. Like therapists, we usually don't know the long-term effects of our work, but every semester I'm confident that more than a few students feel that their lives changed for the better in my class. I don't know whether Donna will remember anything of what she learned about writing, but I'm sure that the insights she gained about her relationship with her father will stay with her because they are so important, which is why she wrote about him in the first place.

Composition teachers quickly develop human as well as professional relationships. Occasionally the easy intimacy of reading and discussing papers about someone else's life and ideas produces dependency or unproductive conflict, but more often such discussion and such relationships leave both students and teacher feeling validated and alive.

For me, the intimacy usually begins as it did with Martin, through music. I grew up with rock and roll and have never lost my taste for it or my desire to explore the latest variations on the old themes. Students list some of their favorite musical groups and songs on their initial questionnaire, and I find a shared interest to discuss in our first conference. Since high school and college males, especially, tend to be fervent about their music and see it as a central part of their identity, musical bonds tend to be strong ones.

But they certainly aren't the only ones. I and other instructors connect with sports, hobbies, hometowns, books, birth order, favorite mountains, phobias, pet peeves, family traumas. Students keep us abreast of campus trends and favorites—from Phish to Julia Roberts to the reemergence of grain alcohol. Exploiting such knowledge and connections for pedagogical purposes is an important part of the writing teacher's art. But just as important, *we* learn and benefit from our intimate connections with composition students.

We connect *ideas*

Reading, events, music, discussion subjects often connect in wonderful and unexpected ways. The day after I use Neil Young's "Down by the River" to talk about the mentality of the girlfriend-blamer, a fourteen-year-old guns down his classmates because a thirteen-year-old has broken up with him, and the next week we read Doris Lessing's short story "A Woman on a Roof," about the rage three roofers feel when a sun-bathing woman on an adjacent roof refuses to acknowledge them. A debate about the value of multi-culturalism ends when a Korean student, Ji-Soo, stuns the class with a convincing presentation about how the definition of "good writing" is culturally determined.

I'm fascinated by connections that show the world as fractals, the whole reflected in the part, the micro a shrunk copy of the macro. The half-hour exercise with which I open the course—students respond to a prompt, go through a process of expanding and reworking their response, then share it with the class—occurs on a larger scale for the next fifteen weeks. The attitudes I see in such an exercise—ranging from intense engagement to aloof superiority—prefigure attitudes I see all semester. The self-image conveyed by that first in-class paragraph appears in every paper thereafter.

We connect *as mentors*

Systematic mentoring of new composition instructors, creating official connections between colleagues, should be a part of every writing program. Mentors can help with Xeroxing on the first day, provide grading tips during finals week, and in between offer stability and reassurance. As mentors, we see our subject with fresh eyes as each new twenty-two-year-old casts off the bowline for the first time. Talking with new instructors helps me see what's new in the composition world and reminds me of old favorite activities that have somehow slipped out of my repertoire. In the absence of any formal mentoring program, developing a mentor relationship with a more experienced instructor may be the most important survival step a new instructor can take. Mentors can lead the way through the department's political maze, suggest how to spend less time on papers, lend the most crucial chapters and articles.

Though we may still be invisible to tenure-track faculty, we daily interact with real people about real subjects in real ways. Sure, we're always playing the teacher role to some degree, and after fourteen years in school, our students know the student role if they know nothing else. But because we learn the details about people that can lead to friendship—about Stefan's search for the perfect guitar tone, for instance, or Steve's volunteering in a shelter for battered women—we easily shed those roles once we turn in the final grades. Not long ago I realized that half of the people I'm still in regular contact with were once my students, and I don't think that's unusual for a composition teacher. I met in my classes the producer of my children's music tapes, my main confidante, my principal anchors to other parts of the world. I make better money when I don't teach, but my life never seems as rich.

We Write

My colleague Mekeel McBride mentioned what sounded like an interesting way to balance the power relations in the writing class: let the students give US an assignment. Intrigued and challenged, I thought, "If Mekeel can do it . . . " and broached the idea to my class, which thought it was a hoot. I left for ten minutes, and when I came back in, I found written on the blackboard, "Write about your first sexual experience." Summoning more courage than I usually need to face a blank page, I wrote what I thought was a respectable and amazingly honest piece, sending a copy to my first sexual partner and reviving a dormant correspondence. The next time I saw Mekeel, I told her about my experience and asked what her class had assigned her to do. "Oh, I haven't done it yet," she laughed. "I just thought it was a good idea."

Seldom does our work assign us a writing task as directly as that class did, but teaching writing can regularly improve our writing productivity, creativity, and content. Certainly teaching takes up time that could be spent writing, and people who believe strongly in their writing often need to drop out of teaching and write full-time. Many composition instructors face the dilemma voiced by Judy Wells's character, The Part-Time Teacher: "Should she stay in the college market and get phobic? Or should she stay in her room like Emily and write poems?" (7).

Teachers who hunger just to write *should* find a way to do it—though good writers often make the best teachers, the feeling "I'd really rather be writing" eventually sours the teaching.

But for those of us who stay hooked on teaching, it doesn't have to be an either/or proposition. The writing class nourishes our writing in important ways.

We write *with inspiration and motivation*

The "invention" work I do in class is among my most inspired, perhaps because of the intensity of doing it in front of an audience, perhaps because I'm a more positive self in class and get interested in more of my ideas than I normally would, censoring fewer than I might in front of my computer monitor. Responding to my own prompt to list traumas, I write "phone phobia," and as I ride the subject through various prewriting steps, it turns to focus on the ways couples divide responsibilities and skills in a marriage. Do we win or lose by taking on some domestic skills and letting others atrophy? I fill the board with quick details and that night write most of a poem, "Splitting the

Difference." It isn't a masterpiece, but it's true *and* my wife likes it, so for me it's valuable writing.

Sometimes writing and pedagogy develop at the same time, quickly making it impossible for us to determine which is the chicken and which the egg. I have students list their writing territories, general subjects they return to time after time— mine include writing, music, teaching, family, the outdoors . . . I explain that it makes sense to exploit several territories at once, since fewer people can write about writing, music, family, *and* teaching, for instance, than can write about any one of those subjects. After such an exhortation one day, I go home and write my own four-territory piece (eventually titled "To Know the Music Is to Reach the Child") and sell it to the *Christian Science Monitor,* which apparently felt I'd found my own niche in the overlapping territories.

The writing class provides writing motivation in a variety of forms, and unless teaching duties overwhelm the writer, teaching can be a productive time. We motivate ourselves by trying out the new assignment we've dreamed up for students. Our students motivate us by writing about subjects or in forms that interest us, challenging us to do the same; by sparking memories or ideas that earn a spot on our "to write" lists; by reminding us of the joy of discovery, the satisfaction of vivid description, the excitement of pursuing an idea to its logical conclusion; by reflecting back to us our own ideas, making us see them in a new light, with more value and promise. I press Tony to explain how he overcame the breakup blues in high school, he returns with a new and much better paper on the evolution of his philosophy, and I'm challenged to write something that similarly links specific personal event and philosophical abstraction.

Our discussions with students, our glimpses into many lives, the brief but sometimes intense relationships that develop, our links with colleagues, felicitous collisions of language that appear in student papers and sometimes on our chalkboards—all can spark a writing blaze. We just have to keep our eyes open for them, give them air when they appear, and find the time to let the blaze burn.

We write *with subjects that teaching offers*

Many composition instructors use their teaching as subject matter, whether for poetry, fiction, essays, or traditional composition scholarship. Occasionally our attempts to explain writers or the writing process turn into valuable pieces of writing themselves. Although I don't always recognize my motivation at the time, I realize in retrospect that many of my poems answer student questions or better explain writing concepts I struggled to articulate in class.

A couple of years ago, for example, I tried to explain to a class what I see as the writer's habit of mind: not an intense search for ideas nor the focus on the day's trivia that occupies most people, but a constant monitoring of what passes by on the conveyor belt of consciousness and, most important, a readiness to yell, "Stop the belt, grab it!" rather than just nod as something interesting passes by. When I started listing the things on my mental conveyor belt and what would make the belt stop, a poem appeared.

Genesis

The brainbelt is a blur:
Mint dental floss
tangled in hair knot clichés,
soggy tissues and old saws,
paper scraps covered with
song lines, badly remembered,
rotting vegetables, the orange and green
now black, squishy,
premasticated,
a bag of cat shit,
cleanly scooped out of the litter,
bagged and forgotten in a corner
until white with redundant mold,
rivers of paper, from glassine to glossy,
thousands of intricately perforated
coupons and inserts
still pouched by grocery ads,
disposable ideas in diapers,
the mundane mile after mile
of bent paper clips, daycamp rules,
shampoo bottles and imitations of McKuen.

Suddenly a sensor trips,
the belt spouts
a shiny flat button
once the eye of a black cotton doggie
whose satiny underear soothed my earliest cheek.

As I've done throughout this book, I borrow ideas, incidents, images from students and their papers. The experiences from which we can draw for our own writing multiply in number and variety as we begin to live vicariously our students' lives.

We write *with practice time shared with our students*

Especially during the first part of a term, many writing teachers give students substantial in-class time to respond to prompts and try out new approaches to their subjects. The prompts come quickly, the writing time never long enough, it seems. Don Murray used to put students through a first day of 90- to 180-second writing bursts, and by the end of the hour, everyone would have a paragraph or two to be proud of. Someone working with relaxed intensity, focused on the task at hand but not expecting anything in particular from it, can accomplish a lot in such short bursts. Bruce Ballenger avoids the tragedy of having to erase all that chalkboard brilliance by using sheets of newsprint for much of his in-class writing.

We write *with new insights into the craft*

Writer-teachers certainly get blocked and frustrated at times as other writers do, and I don't know how one would ever test this hypothesis, but I like to think that writing teachers suffer from fewer psychological writing traumas than do other writers, simply because we know so much about such traumas. We've helped numerous students through writer's block—or convinced them to listen to what the "block" is telling them and postpone writing, gathering more material or doing more prewriting instead. We know that there's a point—I call it the Threshold of Nausea—after which further revision of a piece is impossible without significant time off: we know when to quit. We know that most writers feel they write abnormally slowly, an insight that may help us be more patient.

We see and learn from the weak points in good writers' processes. My wife, Melody Graulich, a prolific, sophisticated, and graceful writer, used to get stuck, frustrated, and angry in the middle of her remarkably final first drafts; her discovery that freewriting could be as helpful in the middle of a process as it is at the beginning taught me to expand my vision of freewriting's uses in my own teaching and writing.

Those of us who collect writers' quotes get a sense of how the great ones have looked at their work. We learn attitudes and habits that we might try to emulate: the necessity of the daily appointment at the writing desk, the importance of discovery as part of the writing process, the habits of observation and notetaking, the joys of tidying up our prose.

Most of us can't claim to churn out the pages while we're teaching and will probably go to our graves wondering what we could have done if we had written full-time, but I feel confident that my day job keeps me filled with subjects and ideas better than any other single aspect of my life.

We Think

My Freshman English class had been pondering their futures, their careers, and I had been trying to get them to take a more active role in preparing for those futures, choosing classes that would help them make decisions or provide them with the knowledge and skills they would need. We read a wonderful Adrienne Rich speech on the subject, brainstormed about what we wanted to be doing in five years, investigated the writing in our majors.

My high school prepared me for taking SATs but not for making decisions, choosing a career, figuring out what I liked or was good at. So as I talked to the confused undeclareds, the second-guessing engineers, musicians torn between playing music and getting a job, I tried to think of what twenty-five years of hindsight has taught me about the way to make such decisions. What advice would I give to my confused undeclared self? On what basis have I made my own decisions?

As I was pondering that issue and planning the rest of my class one night, the answer came to me. People for whom work is more than a paycheck find a job that they like to think about, that engages and absorbs them, that inspires them to be creative and playful—and here I was jotting ideas on my clipboard, involved in all of those ways, enjoying myself.

Much of this book could be called "What we think about when we think about composition." I would guess that the thought involved in teaching composition would vie with the chance to work with so many interesting people as the most important single attraction—for some, addiction—of teaching composition.

We engage in many types of composition-related thought, some of them springing from figuring out how to make the class work. As soon as we finish a day's teaching, sometimes even in the middle of a class, we start thinking about how the next class (or the next time we do this exercise) could be better. Trying to figure out improvements, new ways to reach my students, I think along three major lines:

1. *Putting myself in their shoes.* Sometimes when I imagine what they're feeling, I get transported back to nineteen again, and I remember such things as what a minor role classes played in my life. More often, the exercise makes me realize how different I have become. But in either case, the thinking is engaging.

2. *Connecting the new to the known.* I consider this the most important principle in all education, yet it's one that our educational system ignores with regularity. My use of music is based on this principle—although they often don't know the music I play, students are familiar with thinking about music, "reading" music in certain ways, and I can use that

familiarity to connect to topics from voice to unreliable narrators. As I meander through a semester touching on scores of seemingly unrelated ideas and skills, I try to keep this principle in mind, linking today's tangent to last week's focus.

3. *Responding to the present.* I usually follow Don Murray's advice to throw away all our notes at the end of every course, to avoid repeating ourselves or teaching for last year's students. It's a major challenge to address the students of the moment, concentrate on their problems and strengths, use current examples, but it's a challenge that keeps me fresh and prevents the job from being "same old same old."

Just today a rather depressing moment reaffirmed for me the power of the attraction of composition teachers' thinking. I had been brooding about my first-ever numeric class evaluations—the numbers weren't (need I say it?) as high as I wanted. I couldn't stop thinking about how they called into question my teaching, this book, my reasons for existence. I didn't start to emerge from that particular slough until I could get myself thoroughly engaged in something else—and that something else turned out to be, of course, the next day's class.

3

—

Appreciate Being Off-Track

Backed into a corner by composition instructors angry because the faculty got a raise and the staff got a raise but the instructors got nothing, the tenured director of composition says, "It comes down to supply and demand. I've got a stack of resumes this high on my office desk from people who would love to fill your positions."

In a fourth-floor office after the meeting, several instructors gripe. "I hate it when she starts that 'I've got a stack of resumes this high' routine."

"I especially hate that it's true."

"Yeah, I don't think she likes treating us like shit. I don't think she's got much choice."

"I'd hate to be in her position. We give her a hard time, then she gets put down in eight committee meetings a week because her program doesn't cure student writing or costs too much or takes too many of the TAs."

"I'd rather do a hundred conferences than deal with that shit."

Though composition instructors resent being told by well-paid, tenured professors how lucky they are to have their jobs, not all instructors would jump to tenure-track positions if given the chance. Most faculty members do a lot of onerous, aggravating work for their larger paycheck and job security. We should never stop pushing for better pay and recognition, and some of us may find them only on a tenure track, but to stay sane while waiting for big changes, we should keep in mind the advantages of not being a "real person" in the institution's eyes.

Sometimes it's nice being ignored and invisible. History professors unhappy with their students' writing don't often come huffing up to the fourth

41

floor to find the instructor who actually passed those students in Freshman English the semester before; they're more likely to give the director of composition an earful when they next run into each other at a meeting. We grind our teeth when the department chair doesn't see us as we pass in the hall, but we hope that the chair is equally blind when searching the building for someone to "volunteer" to address the freshman orientation meeting on Saturday.

While most tenure-track faculty spend a painful period each year summarizing and evaluating their year's work and then having everything from the books they teach to their publications scrutinized by a series of committees and administrators, many English departments rehire composition instructors after a cursory glance at their student evaluations, on the basis of reputation or seniority, or even just because it's easier to rehire someone than to comb the files and find someone new. I'm not praising this lax attitude towards instructors—it probably contributes to viewing instructors themselves as lax and disposable—but it does have its benefits.

If you ask tenure-track professors to name the worst part of their jobs, most would say "committee meetings." While few composition teachers can avoid such meetings entirely, they seldom add significantly to our workload, and it's worth reminding ourselves about the burden they put on tenure-track and especially tenured professors. They can absorb more time each week than another class, and they're seldom as pleasant or as productive as a class. The pompous puff up their chests, the macho beat theirs, the dogmatic refuse to budge or listen, the self-absorbed reject the work allotted to them, those enamored with their own voices go on and on and on. They judge curriculum, promotion and tenure, awards, the treatment of human subjects, and job candidates, yet often members leave meetings in despair, feeling that decisions were made for the worst of reasons, the job done more poorly than it would have been by someone working alone.

While I think most composition instructors would do just fine filling professors' shoes in the classroom, many of us would hate being party to painful processes leading to bad choices, compromising with the fatuous, being forced to ignore everything we know about pedagogy and research, making decisions because of fear of lawsuits or to pay back someone else for a dubious favor done years ago, getting caught between the constructionists and the constructivists on a hiring committee, being on the losing side of a terrible vote that "your committee" will get blamed for years into the future.

And though the hoops that instructors have to jump through are often not as paltry as our pay, we don't usually have to kiss up to the dean in cocktail parties, sit through excruciating tenure-committee meetings where people who know nothing about our subject explain how we have to improve to make the grade, or ride the faculty bus around the state, presenting banal oversimplifications of our work to confused alumni.

Ironically, professors go through six years of purgatory to achieve much of the autonomy that we take for granted. Yes, many of our publications are "creative" and therefore ignored by the institution, and even when we do scholarly work it's all but irrelevant to our careers, but not being under the gun of "publish or perish" gives us real freedoms. Unless desperately trying to work their way onto a tenure track, most composition instructors write what they want to write, developing their own poetry or drama or fiction without the self-censoring, the tainted motivation of people writing, in part, to please the institution.

Most of us also have an unusual degree of autonomy in the classroom. We may be given the books to teach, but we can usually select the readings, the approaches, the emphasis, the politics without much fear of someone looking over our shoulders. Even when I had a boss who insisted that I be in the building from 9 to 4, I did what I wanted in the classroom. In most cases, the institution controls only that portion of our time that we spend in class; we make up the rest of our schedule and come and go as we please. Similarly, we go to professional conferences if we want to, not under a heavy sense of obligation; we keep up with the latest scholarship if it interests us, not because we're terrified of senior colleagues finding out that we're behind; we feel little pressure to complicate our classes with teacher research but do it if it intrigues us. If we decide we want to move to Anchorage or Ankara, we can do so without worrying that we're committing professional suicide—and, because our price is low and our skills useful wherever people write English, we can probably find a job.

We do real work with real people writing about real issues. We don't have to volunteer for the fraternity volleyball marathon to feel that we're doing "service"—our entire job is a service. We have a good chance of affecting someone's life rather than producing a report that will get buried among those of other committees, past and present. Neither effete nor overpaid, we can feel some solidarity with the janitor who also works three jobs and shows up at odd hours. We're the working class of the university, and, as John Lennon put it, that's something to be.

4

Work for Systemic Change

Tamara is one of the most talented and energetic teachers I know. She can tease a confession of sensitivity out of a cynical cap-backward frat member. She can get an entire class so involved in a discussion about morality that she has to force them out the door when time's up. Students leave her class wanting to read, to write, to think.

But Tamara has given up teaching everything except the craft at which she now makes a living—creating stuffed bears.

Though Tamara makes great bears, from the perspective of American education, her premature retirement from teaching writing is a tragedy made the more significant because thousands of good teachers join her every year. Many factors influenced Tamara's decision to give up her instructorship, some personal, some professional, but the ones that should worry educators concern her inability to feel valued and respected. The department yawned when she almost single-handedly created and produced an undergraduate literary journal and found outside money to fund it. The college said "no thanks" when I twice nominated her for teaching awards that went to "real" people who have nowhere near Tamara's classroom energy, dedication, or effect.

Tamara is an expert at most of the things I discuss in this book, yet in the end she couldn't live with the system that asked so much of her and gave so little.

I mourn the loss of Tamara—and of Alice and Mark and Becky and countless others—not so much because I care deeply about the quality of education but for selfish reasons: having them around makes me a better, happier teacher. So while I work to make myself more content by practicing the ideas in the rest of this book, I also periodically crusade to change the system, the definition of "instructor" and "full-time," the pay, the benefits, the treatment of writing courses.

In the struggle to improve the jobs of those who teach composition, we can be sure only of the impossibility of generalizing about what "works." In some places, unions embrace part-timers and seem to offer hope for the future; at other schools, unions view nontenure-track instructors as the enemy, threatening the jobs of tenured members. Sometimes working through channels pays off; sometimes only strikes get attention. Tenured English professors may be supportive, indifferent, or downright hostile to us and our attempts to improve our positions. Some departments listen patiently to our pleas and protests; in others, if we complain, we are fired (Ehrenfeld, 12).

Despite such inconsistencies, the instructorship upgrade stories I've read about and participated in lead to some tentative generalizations:

Change (usually) starts at the bottom. Top administrators often change our workload or the requirements we work under, but only the rare, extraordinarily enlightened dean, vice president, or chair undertakes on his or her own the arduous bureaucratic odyssey of materially improving the treatment of nontenure-track teachers. More commonly, the people who need change get together, decide what they want, create a strategy, gather evidence, and try to enlist powerful people for their cause.

The genesis of one of the country's first nontenure-track union bargaining units demonstrates what people can do from the bottom and may serve as a model for similar struggles in other places. One or two extraordinarily dedicated people can make a difference, but their dedication often carries a high personal price.

Christina McVay taught English and German full-time at Kent State University in a nontenure-track position for eleven years before starting a newsletter—*pro-fess-ing*—about nontenure-track issues in 1991. Her local AAUP chapter supported her, letting her use its copy machine. With humor and solid research, she wrote about the inequities and skewed priorities with which all of us are familiar, attacking the administration in ways that won her widespread faculty support. Soon she was sending her biweekly mailings to a huge list of people around the country.

McVay educated and radicalized her constituents; Eric Heller organized them. In 1992, Heller, who taught composition at one of Kent State's campuses, objected when the administration raised his normal teaching load from twelve to fifteen hours per semester. When he became too vocal, he was fired at the end of the 1993 academic year. So he did the footwork, talking to all of the 120 or so full-time, nontenure-track faculty at Kent State, securing the signatures from enough people to force a vote about forming a bargaining unit. The administration pumped out anti-union propaganda, and even the AAUP became jittery, assuring Heller that he wouldn't get the necessary 50 percent approval. But they weren't used to dealing with nontenure-track people, who may be more politicized than their tenure-track peers but, lacking the protection of tenure, learn to keep their mouths shut. Eighty percent voted for the union, which went on to raise substantially the pay of veteran instructors, set a salary floor for new members, establish three-year renewable contracts, and in other ways win for its members the kinds of rights that many American workers take for granted.

At UNH, we risked less and gained less. We periodically begged through appropriate channels, usually with the help of the director of composition. The composition instructorships evolved until by the early 1990s, a dozen of us had three-year renewable agreements, some benefits, five or six courses per year, and salary a little better than half that of untenured assistant professors with five-course loads. We still had to yell to avoid falling through the cracks when they handed out the raises.

The development of the composition program at the University of Nevada, Reno, provides an inspiring exception to the bottom-up pattern. Ann Ronald and Robert Merrill, successive English department chairs, worked for two decades to improve instructor positions. Ronald chronicled their efforts in "Separate but (Sort of) Equal: Permanent Non-Tenure-Track Faculty Members in the Composition Program." Merrill used their experience to write an impassioned critique of CCCC's *Statement of Principles and Standards for the Postsecondary Teaching of Writing* and to sketch an alternative in which "the two tiers" in English departments "fit closer together" (158). Both articles dispel the notion that a nontenure-track "us" must always battle a powerful administrative "them." Both demonstrate that improving the lot of composition instructors is in everyone's best interest.

For years, Reno's English department had to scramble to staff writing courses for rapidly expanding freshman classes. Finally, in 1982, the University created eight full-time, fully funded instructorships, and by the end of the decade, instructors on three-year continuing contracts drew salaries similar to those of local high school teachers, with "full benefits including the possibility of a sabbatical or a professional-development leave" (Ronald, 34). Improvements have continued: a lecturer's teaching load has dropped from four courses to three plus a "service assignment" per semester (while tenure-track faculty teach two), new lecturers now must be paid at least as much as the lowest-paid new assistant professor, and today veteran lecturers make more than some tenure-track faculty members. Lecturers teach a variety of courses, vote in department meetings, have their own offices, and get merit raises.

What does the University of Nevada receive in exchange? A more stable, presumably happier core of composition teachers who publish, head committees, design new programs, write grants and bring in money. One lecturer won a University teaching award, another chaired the faculty senate, another ran the composition program for eight years. Says Ronald, "Essentially, then, not only are the lecturers treated as equals, but they function as equals, performing curricular and extracurricular duties like any other member of the university staff" (34). As Ronald freely admits, the solution itself has caused problems, including resistance towards the lecturers' voting power from tenured professors who either "instinctively view all composition teachers as a lesser order of being" or "naively ignore the changes in the study of rhetoric since [they] were students" (35). Ronald has a number of suggestions for other departments instituting similar programs, but she endorses the concept "unreservedly" (36).

We need to know our strengths. Several times when instructors at UNH organized to demand better treatment, we started by figuring out the actual hours we spent on our classes. The work we do, the importance of our classes to our students, provides our only real leverage. It's worth keeping track of conference hours and papers read, and occasionally we need to articulate exactly what we're trying to do, what we want students to get out of the class. Those faculty annual reports that we rejoice in avoiding might actually help us document our work. Composition courses have hundreds of valid goals, and we need to be ready to articulate them, to account for our hours, to demonstrate the effects we have on students and how much they appreciate us.

We also need to be aware of ways in which the world of education may be catching up to us and beginning to value skills and practices that many of us have long taken for granted. In the opening chapter to his recent collection of articles about teacher education, Frank B. Murray asserts that "The teacher's art is in organizing the activities of the classroom so that the student's work solves a genuine problem that the student brings to the classroom" (9), an art that advocates of open composition assignments have been practicing for decades. In their attention to varieties and complexities of thought, from invention to revision to critical appreciation of literature, composition teachers have also anticipated a demographic change noted by Linda Darling-Hammond and Velma Cobb of the National Center for Restructuring Education, Schools, and Teaching, who write, "the great masses of students now need to be educated for thinking work" (15). Joseph Lowman's exhaustive research into teaching excellence leads him to conclude that the keys to great teaching are qualities most composition teachers possess in abundance: "intellectual excitement" and "interpersonal rapport" with students.

Many professors still cling to the banking concept derided by Paulo Freire, in which the students are turned "into 'containers,' into 'receptacles' to be 'filled' by the teacher. The more completely he fills the receptacles, the better a teacher he is. The more meekly the receptacles permit themselves to be filled, the better students they are" (Freire, 58). But most composition teachers have long believed in student-centered, process-oriented classrooms. When the academic world catches up to its scouts and seers, the treatment of composition instructors will change.

United is the only way to fly. Administrators love to ignore individuals and to respond to our complaints by saying that not everyone chafes under the status quo. If we can't achieve a relatively unified front we should probably forget the whole notion of provoking institutional change. Fighting for change is too time-consuming to take on if it is doomed, though the camaraderie of working together against the common enemy of indifference can bring people together in very positive ways.

With our attention focused on our own plights and those of our immediate colleagues, we may miss important opportunities to work with nontenure-track people in other departments. It's sobering to hear about their conditions and pay, and it reminds us that as badly treated as composition instructors are, our very numbers ensure that we are treated better than adjuncts in some other departments. Yet, ironically, those numbers can make us complacent; at UNH composition instructors began getting yearly raises largely as a result of the efforts of language teachers that none of us had ever met.

Because the strength of solidarity seems indispensable in our struggle, our greatest hope for long-term change rests with unions. McVay and others have found help from the AAUP, though the AAUP chapter at UNH had no energy to expend on nontenure-track woes. The American Federation of Teachers (AFT) went on record in 1979 favoring "pro-rated salaries and fringe benefits" for part-time faculty and staff ("Can We Help . . . [Part 1]," 2), and today it cites an impressive list of "Gains for Part-time and other Nontenure-track Faculty," including improved benefits, greater job security, paid office hours, preference in tenure-track hiring, and eligibility for promotion ("Can We Help . . . [Part 2]"). Yet even the AFT acknowledges that "some members believe . . . that negotiating a salary raise for part-time faculty . . . will strengthen the legitimacy of a hiring trend they bitterly oppose" ("Can We Help . . . [Part 1]," 1). I've known very few composition instructors with the time, energy, and faith in group action that fighting for union representation would require. But if present trends continue, I envision many more instructors turning in desperation to collective action.

We need to face reality. It's foolish to destroy our relationships with chairs and deans over issues they can't control. As Gappa and Leslie demonstrate so well in *The Invisible Faculty,* colleges are currently caught between demands for educational quality and accountability, diminishing education budgets at all levels of government, and a long-term trend in many universities that emphasizes research and devalues teaching. In the words of Glassick, Huber, and Maerhoff, "The academy . . . began to undervalue teaching just as the changing profile of the student body made the need for good teaching both more important and more challenging" (8). The tensions between these contradictory trends are national in scope and seem to call for national attention, yet the only aspects of education politicians seem interested in are testing, technology, and finding new ways to allow rich kids more choice.

So deans and chairs are, and for the foreseeable future will be, in a squeeze. Since they can more easily fire, burden, or manipulate powerless, "part-time" instructors than take something away from tenured professors, it's only logical that they're grudging with what they give us and eager to take back any time they can. Even administrators with the best intentions may find it impossible to overcome resistance, tradition, and inertia in the department or the college. I doubt many administrators have done all that they can to improve the conditions under which composition instructors work; Judy Wells did not have to strain her imagination to create the administrator who magnanimously grants The Part-Time Teacher the right to make her class ten extra Xeroxes (5). But we need to keep in mind that "all that they can do" may not be much.

Despite this gloomy picture, long-term educational change may favor composition instructors. At the moment, many universities, run by people who came of age viewing tenure as the savior of Western intellectual thought, seem bent on protecting the select few who made it inside the academy walls before the drawbridge went up. Yet as the contrast sharpens between some older, tenured professors, intellectually exhausted and coasting, and energetic young hotshots for whom the academy has no room, more and more people question the value of tenure. And while academics debate that value, institutions themselves seem bent on making tenure obsolete. Nontenured faculty already teach a majority of the courses at community colleges throughout the country, and if current trends continue, tenure-track faculty will soon become a minority throughout post-secondary education, except at small liberal arts colleges. (See, for instance, the National Center for Educational Statistics' report, *The Condition of Education,* 186-187.) Once the concern only of groups like the AAUP and the CCCC, this trend now worries readers of such mainstream media as *The New Republic* (Hickman), and accrediting agencies are beginning to complain about schools' adjunct-to-faculty ratio.

The CCCC calls the relegation of so many writing teachers to part-time and/or temporary appointments "the worst scandal in higher education to-day" (*Statement,* 1). The CCCC (and, as far as I can see, everyone else who has studied the issue) asserts that the poor treatment of nontenure-track faculty is morally and educationally unjustifiable and calls for the treatment of non-tenure-track people to parallel more closely that afforded those on the tenure line. While some educational commissions and the popular media fret that nontenure-track or part-time teachers provide students with an inferior edu-cation (one "study group" concluding, for instance, that "one full-time fac-ulty member is a better investment than three part-timers" [cited in Gappa and Leslie, 5]), Gappa and Leslie develop a spirited defense of nontenure-track teachers, arguing what many of us know—that nontenure-track faculty are often more dedicated to teaching than are their tenured, research-oriented peers, and they bring to their teaching fresh, up-to-date ideas gleaned from their work outside the academy.

The growing number of nontenure-track faculty makes tenured faculty understandably nervous. Yet as Gappa and Leslie put it, "The reason for the two faculties is that the one sustains the other: the low costs and heavy under-graduate teaching loads of the have-nots help make possible the continuation of a tenure system that protects the jobs and the perquisites of the haves" (2). Administrators are often quick to capitalize on the rift between the two groups. But it seems clear that in the long run, everyone would benefit from improving the treatment of instructors. As McVay says, none of us will pro-gress "if tenured faculty allow administrations to use and abuse nontenured faculty." By standing up for the rights of people not in the tenure line, tenure-track faculty ultimately protect their own rights. Our joint goal should be not ridding the university of nontenure-track teachers but extending the benefits and protections of tenure to all teachers. As the AFT says, "Improving the pay, benefits, and working conditions of part-time and nontenure-track faculty may turn out to be the only way to cure the addiction of administrators to this form of cheap labor" ("Can We Help . . . [Part 1]," 1).

Although the general trends in higher education have increased the numbers of composition instructors without improving our treatment, that may change under continued public scrutiny and calls for accountability. Most universities have circled the wagons to protect tenured faculty and bloated administrations, but I think eventually they will have to justify them-selves by reference to one of two models. If they follow the traditional "we do education" model and start evaluating courses and teachers based on how much they educate, not how much grant money they generate or how much scholarship they publish or how long they've been around, composition in-structors stand to benefit. In Barry Greer's words, universities will have to "put a little of that lottery money into low tech, into keeping skilled writers in higher education, skilled writers who teach what they do best" (79).

If, on the other hand, universities fall prey to market thinking and accept profit as the only legitimate goal, they have to justify themselves on a business model. A business faced with downsizing would keep the classes that produce a lot of education for small paychecks and get rid of classes in which a $70,000/year full professor teaches six students Chaucer or postmodern postcolonial theory. Again, instructors stand to gain.

I'm not saying these trends are good: they outline a future in which all faculty are like service employees, called in to flip a burger "just-in-time." We daily confront the negative effects of tenure, but the alternative—to put all "educational" power in the hands of administrators and legislators—would almost certainly be worse. A long-term goal for composition instructors, then, is to convince their more powerful colleagues that we all rise or fall together. As the AFT says, "Full-time faculty must regard part-time faculty as colleagues in the academic community" (*Statement*, 8). Lending everyone copies of *The Invisible Faculty* would be a good first step.

5

—

Consider Alternatives

Fresh out of college with a degree in English, Paul traveled by thumb around South America, earning enough to support himself and his Brazilian girlfriend by teaching and tutoring English. These days he still travels a lot, but in somewhat easier conditions—companies like Apple and FedEx fly him around the world to give training seminars.

Barry used to be the most eccentric person on our writing staff. No one knew how he would get by when he lost his job—I think administrators wondered whether his class did any work between listening to Barry play the guitar and getting inspiration for wacky stories from his collection of photographs and drawings. Now groups and companies around the country pay Barry more for a day of his eccentric writing exercises and advice than he used to make for teaching an entire semester of Freshman English.

Joe was a dedicated fiction writer and outstanding teacher, working on his novel between conferences. A computer company lured him away, and instead of racking up Pulitzers, he wins awards for his great software manuals.

Barbara began supplementing her instructor's income by counseling students a few hours per week in the dean's office. She liked the work and the unquestioning sense of respect she felt from students and administrators alike, and when a full-time counselor's job opened up, the dean made her an offer she couldn't refuse.

For those of us who spent years struggling through graduate school and/ or putting in time at the bottom of the university's pecking order, the idea of giving it all up, turning our backs on college teaching, provokes significant cognitive dissonance. If I leave the university, won't the last fifteen years be wasted? The issue becomes even more fraught with emotional trauma for those of us who have spent our whole lives involved with education. We know no other life; for us, "alma mater" is not just a Latin name for the school song.

For such people (and I'm one of them; I've never spent a full year away from classrooms) contemplating alternatives can be tremendously liberating after the initial fear wears off. There IS life outside the university, and it can take pleasant, challenging, and financially rewarding forms, as the people whose stories begin this chapter would be glad to confirm. One phone call, one contact can produce more improvement in our professional situation than a lifetime of petitioning the dean.

Teaching

Private sources provide more than 40 percent of the funding for post-secondary education (National Center for Educational Statistics, "Indicator 41," 1), and many of the classes paid for by such funds take place outside of traditional academic settings. If trends continue, with colleges forever trimming every budget but the football team's, businesses will need to hire more and more in-house trainers and outside consultants. To fill some such jobs, writing teachers need new training in such things as time management, computer technologies, public speaking, ESL. But people with years of classroom experience have the basic skills to work with trainees (who aren't very different from students) and to learn quickly themselves. Some of the most successful ex–English teachers I know spent a year or two adding another skill to their repertoire and now star in the world of corporate training.

But there is also a lot of work that requires nothing beyond the skills we already have. Businesses have been saying for years, "We can teach them the business; we just can't teach them to write," and business leaders who can see beyond tomorrow's balance sheet recognize the long-term value in improving employees' writing and thinking skills. I was lucky enough to work for such a leader in an insurance company. He not only saw the value of writing training, he recognized the importance of slow, steady work and let me set up a ten-week "semester." Less enlightened heads of human resource development insist on a one- or two-day writing retreat, which they imagine will solve all of their company's writing problems. Such immersion therapy doesn't make much pedagogical sense, but it's surprisingly easy to adapt for more extended workshops the methods we've developed for fifty- or eighty-minute classes.

Like many academics, I was in for some surprises when I first ventured outside the ivy walls. The competitiveness and constant focus on the bottom line that I associate with American business didn't have any effect on the people I worked with. Unquestionably adult, not late adolescents choosing between a night of writing and a night of beer, they often fully appreciated what I had to offer and found my methods and my subject a relief after the tedium of their jobs.

The highest-profile, potentially highest-paying alternative to traditional college teaching is full-time consulting, giving workshops for groups of teachers or wannabe writers, flying around the country, hawking one's own books or videos. Breaking into that world involves a certain amount of chutzpa or desperation, a good stage presence, and luck or contacts. But it can be done.

Though career consultants and best-sellers gladly take our money to advise us about making the leap between the academic and business worlds, we all know the "secrets": get your name onto executives' desks, develop a reputation, milk contacts. Find out which local businesses hire university-affiliated people—perhaps accountants or computer experts—talk to those accountants, find out who they work with. Give workshops through continuing education in business writing or computers-and-writing and talk to the companies that your students work for. Pick the brains of deans or whoever deals with "outside world" contacts at your university. Businesses often know they need help but don't know where to get it, so they blindly send out pleas to local colleges. Work with local business schools or M.B.A. programs. You never know which of your students is going to make it big and want to hire you.

Writing

As an undergraduate, I figured I would need to teach to support my writing habit, but for a good portion of my professional life, I have written to support my teaching habit. There is a lot of work out there for people who can produce clear, lively, concise writing, especially if they can do it quickly. Downsized publishers no longer have enough in-house writers and editors, so they need people to write the boxes and sidebars that add interest to textbooks, to turn into readable English the plodding prose of their content experts, to create the endless ancillaries—workbooks and test questions and mini-magazines—that help sell their textbooks. Our skills and our ideas, which colleges regularly undervalue, often seem new and exciting—even magical—to business consultants or organizations trying to spread their messages.

Again, contacts and name recognition produce most first jobs in the world of nonacademic writing, but even the most unlikely tactics work on occasion. Scour the walls of English departments for "help wanted" notices. (Thanks to such a notice, I once made a thousand dollars writing a book about people named "Brown.") Send query letters to publishers; you never know when your letter will land on someone's desk just when that someone is tearing her hair over the unreadability of what she hoped would be a best-selling text.

Current technology makes writing for hire much more feasible and attractive than it was twenty years ago. It doesn't matter where you live as long as there's a phone line or a FedEx box nearby. Though they're skimpy on personnel, publishers seem to love to spend money on overnight delivery, if they haven't yet started transferring all their material over phone lines.

Note that I'm not advocating starting a new career as a traditional freelance writer, querying editors about story ideas or writing and submitting articles. Some people do live that way, generally people who have developed a particular expertise—in science writing or travel writing, say—and whose name means enough to editors in their field that their articles always find a home and command a substantial price. People just starting out will find steadier, more certain income doing the writing others want, rather than trying to convince someone to buy the writing they've done or want to do.

Going Tenure-track

Yes, it's possible. Composition instructors can go back and get a Ph.D. or focus all their writing energy on composition articles. I don't know anyone who has retooled him- or herself and then found a tenure-track job at the same institution, but I know a couple of people who evolved from poorly treated, poorly paid instructors at one institution to highly respected members of another institution in just a few years—one actually jumped directly to writing program administrator.

To pursue any of these alternatives, we must first convince ourselves of our own value, something that our previous treatment can make very difficult. It's easy to get overwhelmed by the sheer numbers of our competition, all the other people out there with master's or Ph.D.s in English looking for better work or for any work at all. But as Sandra Cisneros says, we need to write about (or use) what makes us different. Not many of those thousands of out-of-work English graduates have experience in business writing, or a knack for making groups laugh and compromise, or an ability to explain relativity so that others can understand it, or an interest in making, not just using software, or an aunt who's a senior editor at a New York publishing house.

As I write this, I hear readers asking, "So why aren't you out there making your millions in the nonacademic world?" I have orbited universities for my entire professional life, sometimes making twice my present salary writing, appearing in the ivy-covered buildings only to keep my face familiar. But I'm lucky enough not always to need the higher pay of the business world—my spouse is a full professor, relatively well paid—and I find that I keep coming back to teaching writing because of all the factors I discuss in this book.

6

Lower Stress and Anxiety

Even I knew there was no point in checking my materials—books, overheads, handouts—another time. And standing outside the classroom door in the antiseptic hall, tensely waiting for the magic moment when "my" class would assemble itself for the first time, seemed like psychological suicide. So I walked blindly down to the other end of the hall and found a door leading out into a courtyard, where I could take loud deep breaths and keep my feet moving. After I'd paced the yard a dozen times, the door opened, and a secretary I had just met that morning, looking cool and calm in a summer dress, stared at me with a half-concerned, half-amused expression and asked, "What's wrong with you?"

Sounding, I'm sure, like I'd been wound too tight, I answered, "I'm about to teach my first class!"

I've since experienced so many moments of first-day jitters that I probably would have forgotten that one except that the contrast between the secretary's aplomb and my terror was so deliciously ironic, given our relative status in the educational system. After twenty-three years, first-day stress has transformed into the pleasant, energetic high of taking the stage once again, searching a roomful of new faces, wondering what they have in store for me. Other sources of anxiety more specific to composition teaching continue to haunt me from time to time, but I've found many ways to reduce the overall stress and anxiety of the job. Although we have plenty of rational reasons to feel anxious while teaching composition, exposing ourselves and our knowledge to constant scrutiny, handling students' current crises and scars and wounds from the past, passing judgment and handing out grades in a discipline with admittedly subjective stances and answers, we *can* transform teaching writing into a low-stress occupation. While virtually all of the suggestions in this book have stress reduction as a secondary goal, this chapter focuses directly on some of the most common sources of stress and anxiety and suggests ways to reduce their effect on us.

Make our teaching consistent with our values

Many sources of anxiety for the writing teacher spring from deep-seated conflict between our beliefs and the activities we engage in, especially when external requirements dictate what we do. Luckily for me and my students, I have never been forced to teach students to diagram sentences or identify parts of speech. But my recent experience teaching "Research Writing," feeling obligated to deal with citation formats, gave me some practice in maintaining my sense of integrity while teaching something that the institution values more highly than I do. I let students know that I think the only important part of citations is content, the research trail, and we treated the endless picky questions about parenthesis and period placement as a game—not an irrelevant, stupid game, but a game nevertheless.

Perhaps others would consider it unprofessional of me to break ranks with the program, the department, or the university and take, to some extent, the students' "side." I consider it unprofessional—and unfair to students— to fabricate allegiance to others' values, to lie about what I consider important. If I pretend that I think the placement of the publication date in a citation is as serious an issue as, say, the need for quotation marks around someone else's sentence, I give my students a warped sense of values that could lead them both to distrust my judgment and to make significant ethical errors of their own.

To ensure that our courses express our values, Leaf Seligman suggests that as we plan our courses we should take a systematic look at our beliefs and the readings we use in class. She writes down her general beliefs, her teaching beliefs, and her teaching objectives for a writing class, then analyzes each reading to see which objectives each contributes to. She tries to avoid holding on to sentimental favorites that don't do the work she wants her readings to do.

Such a process can help us weed out readings and exercises that work for someone else but that don't really fit in our courses. Although I'm a firm believer in trading ideas and activities with colleagues, such borrowing can add to our anxiety. We need to make borrowed activities *ours*. No matter how well something might have worked for a colleague, if we don't fully understand it or can't work up enthusiasm for it or simply don't have the right personality for it, it may fail miserably in our class. Poet friends report fun, productive classes growing out of metaphors built from random combinations of a word from a "concrete" list and one from an "abstract" list, but when I try such an approach, I find that the class's reaction mirrors mine: That's amusing, but where does it get us? We need to consider all such borrowings experiments, more likely to work the second or third time, after we've found ways to put our stamp on them.

We usually have an easier time spotting clashes between our beliefs and external pressures than we do seeing the inconsistency between some of our own practices and our beliefs. We all do some things in class because we've always done them or because our teachers did them. It's worth ferreting such things out of our classes, asking whether they serve a purpose that we still find worthwhile.

Perhaps, for instance, we still give students grammar drills or have them study spelling "rules" or work their way through the library's endless self-study exercise. We apologize when we make the assignment but feel it's one of those things we just have to do. We need frequent self-scrutiny and research to ascertain whether we *do* have to do it, whether doses of this particular castor oil make the patient better. The evidence against grammar drills, isolated from a writing context, is quite convincing. And while I haven't researched the issue of teaching spelling, I think spell-checkers have made it almost a nonissue; perhaps what we need to teach now is how to learn from your spell-checker (and how to recognize and differentiate among homophones). Learning to use something complex—like a library, a computer, or a word processing program—almost always involves some trial and error, some wasted time, some frustration, but if we examine the processes, we can eliminate the true busywork and help students create an interesting, personal goal so that they will see the frustration as being in the service of something valuable. Instead of completing a generic library exercise that requires learning how to use the microfilm reader, students can look up their birthday in the *New York Times;* instead of each individual in class gradually puzzling out the library's idiosyncrasies, we can hold a "tips" session in which we swap insights about waiting shelves, recall policies, and reliable copy machines.

Similarly, it's worth asking if we're really grading what we want to grade, evaluating what we believe are the most important aspects of student writing and performance. I have argued (in "In Defense of Subjective Grading") that subjective grading of papers is not only defensible but desirable, since writers almost always write for particular, idiosyncratic audiences. If students can learn to write up to our standards of "good writing," they can probably adjust to the standards of the next professor or boss. To make such subjectivity defensible, however, we must make our standards as explicit as possible, so that students can practice meeting them, not spend the whole term trying to figure out what they are. The teacher who has been as open, direct, and specific about grading standards as possible shouldn't feel guilty about not being "objective."

But just because we have articulated and explained our standards doesn't necessarily mean we believe in them. During my first quarter of teaching, a respected senior colleague told me that he never gave above a C+ to a paper that included a sentence fragment or run-on, and I followed his lead for years—announcing my stand to my students—before I questioned whether such errors should negate all of a paper's strengths. I also tend to be too ruled by numbers, meticulously averaging a student's paper grades according to the formula in my syllabus, afraid to be swayed by gut feelings. And sometimes I have to remind myself that paper length alone means nothing.

I list these examples not to change the criteria anyone uses for grading papers but to suggest the lines of thinking that might help others lower their anxiety about grading. When I analyze why I'm stressed about a particular grade, I usually find that I don't really believe in it, I've been too inflexible, swayed by a "should" or an "ought," and to feel better I need to find the underlying clash of values and try to eliminate it.

Classroom anxiety can also spring from our sense that we have had to shed our politics at the door or that we're being more or less directive than we'd like to be. I've had good teachers who ranged across the authoritarian spectrum. Teachers I had trouble with tended to be those who gave mixed messages, often appearing to be loose and accepting but with unexpected moments of rigidity, taking two points off for every spelling mistake or insisting (in a boys' prep school) that every tie be tight, even while claiming to consider ties absurd.

Politics in the classroom is a touchy issue; I struggle constantly over how many of my own political beliefs I can legitimately import into the class. I'm clearer on the need to be honest—maybe when everyone else has spoken—about my opinion on issues that arise in class discussion. If I think an idea is sexist, I'll say so. If someone brings up the National Rifle Association, I'll say I hold it responsible for every gun death in America, but I encourage students to disagree with me, and the last pro-gun paper I received got the highest grade in the class. I'm not so much interested in swaying my students' opinions as I am in not taking on the stress of hypocrisy. The ability of student and teacher to accept each other's opinions is an important aspect of classroom trust and an important facet of the bond between them. "To trust means not just to tolerate a variety of viewpoints, acting as an impartial referee, assuring equal air time to all. It means to try to *connect*, to enter into each student's perspective" (Belenky et al., 227).

Believe in what we do

Few things depress me more than feeling as though I've sacrificed time and foregone income for nothing, and writing teachers who hear only gripes and see only failures often end up at the Prozac dispensary. We need to arm ourselves with all the evidence we can muster that shows that our work works.

Reading can help, although we need to select carefully. I don't gain much validation from diving headlong into *College English* or *College Composition and Communication;* I often find myself drowning in articles that I consider unreadable, that are not interested in the actual practice of writing, and that are determined to demonstrate the intellectual vacuity of people who disagree with the author. The idea that the composition community can be a cooperative, sharing place, rather than a competitive, divisive world has only recently begun filtering up to the top journals.

Similarly, I avoid writers who seem enamored with theory, the history of composition, and rhetoric. People in these fields obviously have made tremendous contributions to the work we do, but at the moment we're looking for readings that will confirm our sense of efficacy, not make us feel suicidal because of our ignorance of Cicero.

I'm cheered and empowered by writers who focus on students, the classroom, and the acts of writing, reading, and teaching. Constance Weaver and Rei Noguchi, grammarians who write for the rest of us, provide strong evidence of what works and doesn't work. Donald Murray is my favorite composition writer because of his lucidity, his generosity towards writers, teachers, and students, his focus on what writers actually do, his enthusiasm for his subjects. Countless others share many of Murray's traits and send teachers back to the classroom with renewed enthusiasm—Janet Emig, Ken Macrorie, Peter Elbow, Linda Rief, Nancie Atwell, Ralph Fletcher, Tom Romano, Bruce Ballenger, Donald Graves.

We can consult these writers to provide a direction, backbone, or justification for each move we make in our classrooms. I remember feeling embarrassed about the lack of planned progression or coherence in my classes until Dan Reagan, then a graduate student, pointed out that the logical movement of any writing class mirrors the process of writing a single paper, starting with ways of coming up with topics and ending with proofreading and publication. I've now created a thousand variations of Dan's theme, and I still find the central advice compelling. Reading a book like Tom Romano's *Writing with Passion* both confirms and validates some things I do instinctively and stretches those instincts—particularly about the place of fiction and poetry in our classes.

Every composition instructor should read Susan H. McLeod's chapter "Endings: Teacher Affect/Teacher Effect," which presents considerable research to affirm the value of our work. After discussing how teachers' expectations, attitudes, and practices can create either a "Pygmalion effect" or a "Golem effect," lead students to believe in either their abilities or their hopelessness, McLeod focuses on two attributes of teachers who contribute to more Pygmalions than Golems.

- **Empathy.** McLeod quotes Elbow—"liking . . . leads to improvement" (McLeod, 113)—and summarizes Eccles and Wigfield's definition of "a warm, supportive classroom atmosphere: deemphasize evaluations and minimize competition, set high but realistic expectations, communicate the conviction that all students can master the material, and express the belief that the material is worth mastering" (McLeod, 113–114). She concludes that students at every level improve when taught by empathic teachers who "actively engage themselves in the thinking and learning processes of their students" (McLeod, 114).
- **Teachers' Self-Efficacy.** If we think that students can improve and that we can help them, we're likely to be right on both counts.

Along with amassing theory and research showing that our methods *should* work, we obviously need to confirm that they *do* work. I'm not talking about digging up standardized test scores or surveys of today's student writing compared to that of ten or a hundred years ago—though interesting, those can seldom affect the way we feel about this particular class this particular semester. We can find better evidence every day.

With everything else that writing teachers have to pay attention to, we may forget to look for the best data while we still have a chance. Then we fall back on official student evaluations, often unsatisfying sources of self-confirmation. We're better off keeping our eyes open throughout the term for the following:

- **Improved Papers.** Sometimes it's hard to separate the changes we suggested from ones that students make on their own, but most students, given the chance to revise and some pointers about how to do it, make the paper at least somewhat better. It may be worth keeping a copy of the first draft a student hands in to highlight improvement and to reassure ourselves if the student's final portfolio still leaves us groaning.
- **Self-reports.** Occasionally, generous or sensitive students let teachers know how the class has affected them. I appreciate enormously such confirmation, but I get more consistent self-reports from the last paper in each course, a writing self-analysis. I assign the paper to get students

to think about themselves as writers and especially to confess their strengths and make resolutions about their weaknesses. But even when students don't consciously address the effects of the class, it's usually easy to infer from their own confessions about their writing that the class has opened their eyes, changed their attitudes, given them new strength or confidence. The assignment pays off for everyone.

- **Third-person Reports.** Composition teachers tend to be a close-knit group because we all share the need for self-affirmation and we're constantly on the lookout for ways to provide it for others. So when a student reports that Alice's Freshman English class inspired her to be an English major, I let Alice know. Out of such gossip reputations grow, and some of us rely on reputations to take the place of titles and endowed chairs.

When we lack such evidence of our positive influence, and despite student complaints about "I don't know what you want" or "I don't get it," we should be confident of our effect in a number of areas. Students given a course-long dose of process methods will almost certainly retain the idea that there's more than one way to write a paper, and those even slightly engaged by process approaches will remember and possibly even use a couple.

Though a student's papers may show no vast improvement, any positive change in the student's attitude towards writing should be considered a major victory, a sign that the course had value. Attitude, I contend, is the single most important factor in writing. With a bad attitude, a writer will never advance beyond minimal effort and minimal production—and a huge proportion of students come to college with a bad attitude towards writing.

Even if a student's attitude shows no significant change during the class, we can retain hope in the long term because we give students better experiences with writing than they're likely to have had before. If students write one essay they really care about, get one enthusiastic response from teacher or classmates, read one piece of writing they really like, in the long run their view of English classes and writing may improve, since few students report having had such experiences before they got to college.

Be ourselves

I argue elsewhere in this book that both we and our students benefit from our being as comfortable, honest, and real as possible in the classroom. We shouldn't feel that we're putting on masks to deal with students; it takes energy to hold a mask on, and eventually that strain turns into anxiety. Obviously we can't show to a class everything about us that family and friends see, but if we avoid the kind of falseness I discuss at the beginning of this chapter, we can see ourselves as simply letting some parts of our personality get the spotlight while others take a breather.

Even a hint of falseness can be the pea under the mattresses, leaving us sleepless and worried. The most lucrative teaching job I've ever had was working with fifteen information systems experts of a big insurance company for two hours per week. Often relieved to be manipulating words not numbers and to be talking to a different set of people, my students generally enjoyed the class, and I liked them: they were bright and attentive students and good writers. It was probably the easiest teaching I've ever done, and at one point I figured I was earning seventeen times more per hour in that sterile conference room than I was getting chalk dust on my clothes in basement classrooms and offices at the University. Yet after doing it for six years, I still wasn't comfortable; the week's anxiety always focused on that class. I still broke into that first-day sweat when I had to put on a tie, ask the security guard to call my contact, worry if a teleconference had taken over my seminar room, hope someone hadn't used permamarkers on the white board. Putting on that bit of a mask always felt like a burden.

It's worth asking ourselves how we're different in- and outside class and what those differences mean. For me such an analysis leads me to resolve to export more of my classroom self into the "normal" me: he's more confident, more articulate, more ready and able to show off, wittier (at least if the audience responds), more accepting. The classroom persona's shortcomings are carefully controlled and appropriate: he's less sexual, less political, less opinionated, less cynical.

"Being ourselves" applies to what we read and write in our classes as well. I teach only readings about which I'm so enthusiastic that I can carry the whole class, if necessary. I see no point in undermining my enthusiasm by teaching books and essays I don't care about. Of course I work to keep the list fresh and full of books by people who are not *like* me; I continue to expand my interests and tastes, but I don't feel a need to adopt someone else's.

I also strive to write about real subjects when I'm doing on the board an assignment my students are completing on paper. Only by addressing my own real concerns am I likely to come up with the kind of productive tangent that might spark my writing and that I want to model for students. I get a fair amount of real writing and thinking done in the classroom, and my students appreciate watching me go through various moods as I write—puzzled, surprised, delighted, confused, frustrated, contemplative.

Students tend to see my musical choices as the most direct door into who I am, and though students often appear to be ignoring the music, they comment on it more than on any other aspect of my classes. On days when I don't haul my boom box to class, I open the session with "Tales from the Out-side World," retelling briefly a news item I've heard or read, revealing what matters to me in the outside world. Sometimes if the class doesn't go well, I comfort myself by saying "At least they're going away knowing more about East Timor or GATT than they did this morning."

Recognize that the field is full of contradictions

Since first discovering that every issue in composition has two appealing but contradictory solutions, every piece of advice is balanced by its opposite, I have tried to, in Peter Elbow's terms, embrace the contraries, revel in the feel-ing of being tugged in two directions. With F. Scott Fitzgerald, we need to "hold two opposed ideas in the mind at the same time, and still retain the abil-ity to function" (69). Composition teachers do well to keep in mind the com-plex nature of the discipline; otherwise, the first time they find themselves telling one student to complicate a paper's thinking and the next student to simplify, they may decide to retire.

Among the most common apparent contradictions: We encourage students to be *clear,* which generally entails providing ample explanations and details, but we also want them to be *concise.* We've learned to honor the *process,* but we still grade the *product.* We know that giving students intensive *help* makes their papers better, but we also want them to become *their own best editor,* not dependent on anyone's help. We want to *validate their unique-ness* but also help them with *practical skills* they need to get along. We want to *value* who and where they are but also help them *change* and grow. We want them to be *creative* and original, but we also usually insist that they use *con-ventional* punctuation and grammar.

Any teacher could compile a list of such conundrums. Though in fact we often manage to do *both*—write clearly *and* concisely, for instance—we need to be able to explain to students that the sense of being pulled in two direc-tions is an unavoidable part of our discipline but not a logical cul-de-sac. Yes, the writer struggles between Scylla and Charybdis, but that's what makes writ-ing such a challenging odyssey.

Accept the limitations of likely change

During my first year at UNH, old-timers kindly explained to me the twelve-week rule, also known as Carnicelli's rule, after the colleague who first articu-lated it. The rule asserts that no matter what you do in class or how you set up the course, many students won't begin to show noticeable change until week twelve of a fifteen-week semester. Anticipating such results can keep comp teachers from pulling out their hair at midterm. And it's certainly not the only reality of college life over which we have no control but which nevertheless undermines our effectiveness:

- Though we can motivate many students and even successfully light fires under a few, inevitably some of our students are too young or too thoughtless or too tired or too hungry or too distracted to pay serious attention, no matter what the subject.

- Many departments view composition classes as a necessary evil, something their majors just have to get checked off their lists, and they make it clear that students should put their serious efforts into classes in their major.

- Some excellent students work forty-hour jobs and have families to boot. Though they often manage their time better than their unemployed peers, sometimes they simply don't have the time to do their best work.

- Long before students get to college, their language training has been affected by a host of psychological and cultural factors—varieties of intelligences, cultural definitions of "good writing," scars and beliefs from years of English classes. We can't hope to understand or make allowance for all such factors.

We've got enough to work on without struggling against the inevitable or wrestling with the insurmountable. We need at least to entertain the possibility that "it's not my fault." Janet Emig labels "magical thinking" the whole notion "that children learn *because* teachers teach" (135). She argues that because humans develop writing ability naturally, writing teachers should focus on providing an "enabling environment"—"safe, structured, private, unobtrusive, and literate," with "frequent opportunities to practice writing, many of these playful." We need to be "fellow practitioners, and . . . providers of possible content, experiences, and feedback" (139). Much of the rest is up to the student.

Remember the primacy of attitude

Keeping in mind what we really want students to get out of our classes can simplify our lives and reduce the stress of realizing that MaryAnn hasn't learned semicolons and Reggie still can't write a paper with a point. What determines whether the class was worthwhile for a student and therefore for us? For me, the answer is attitude. If students' attitudes towards writing improve, if they fear it less, hate it less, see it as less alien, they're more likely to procrastinate less, get help more often, see writing as a way to express and learn rather than a tool of evaluation and punishment. Most students come into my classes on a long downward spiral in their attitude towards writing—a bad experience led them to dislike writing, which made them procrastinate and put less effort into it, which produced worse results and grades, a bad experience that led to more procrastination . . . If I can reverse that spiral, even if I don't see any results, I feel I've been successful.

As proof of the primacy of attitude, I think of Ant, a Thai student I worked with. His English was shaky, and we struggled along on basic issues, but he was always cheerful, optimistic, and hard-working. One day he came in bursting with excitement; he'd found the book he'd been looking for, the book that showed him what he needed to know about English sentences. It was Joseph Williams' *Style,* a great book that I happened to be using in my Prose Writing class, where some of the native English speakers regularly moaned about its overly sophisticated analysis. Ant's English was uneven, but his attitude was advanced, and I bet he's now fluent and confident.

I have taught for years with Shannon, long enough to see patterns among her ex-students. In my judgment, they often don't write very well, but they have tremendous enthusiasm for reading and writing, they voraciously gobble up Shannon's favorite author (Raymond Carver), and they're giddy with the resolution that English is their future. Sometimes it's difficult to let these students know that they still have much to learn, but they uniformly view Shannon as having given them a tremendous gift, a new way to perceive writing and reading.

We have a variety of different gifts to offer students, from new ways to understand poetry to word processor secrets. Our class has succeeded if all that students take away from it is a new feeling about words.

7

Limit Our Sense of Responsibility

It was the last day of finals in eighth grade. Our science teacher, Mr. Shuman, came bouncing in to hand out his exam, full of his usual ebullience, a bright red bow tie symbolizing his jaunty attitude toward the day. Maybe he sensed the somberness of the rest of us, for by the time he'd reached the last row, he'd slowed down considerably, and when he arrived at the final, empty desk, and stood with the extra exam in his hand, clouds of confusion had settled in his face.

"I could have sworn I counted them out right," he mumbled as our home-room teacher, his face already asking forgiveness from the old man, took Mr. Shuman by the arm and led him out into the hall to tell him that the missing student, Ned, had the night before tied a plastic bag around his head. When Mr. Shuman came back in, his shoulders were slumped, he'd aged immeasurably, his face was drained. The jauntiness was forever gone.

I hope I never stand in the shoes of that kindly old science teacher, wondering if my class had driven a kid to suicide. But I think any composition instructor doing a decent job wrestles constantly with issues of responsibility: Where does my job end and the student's take over? I would not want to teach in a situation where I was forbidden to get involved in my students' lives; such involvement produces many of the benefits that this book celebrates. But we run a real risk of getting too involved and carrying the weight of fifty or seventy-five lives. So I offer the following suggestions in the hope that they may help other instructors avoid feeling the way Mr. Shuman did.

We should coach, not profess

Writing teachers have plenty to talk about, and like professors in any subject, we could easily lecture our way through entire semesters, engaging in what Paulo Freire calls the "banking" view of education. But if we expound on the brilliance of the day's reading and lay before the class our pearls of experiential wisdom about writing, we inevitably face frustration when we find students blind to the brilliance, indifferent to the pearls, bored of being receptacles. Writing is a skill more than a body of knowledge, and both we and students suffer when we ignore the distinction.

Because it's a skill, writing is best treated like a sport or a craft—tennis or cabinetmaking, for instance. And writing teachers, no matter what their status, need to think of themselves not as people who profess but as coaches or master craftspeople, watching their apprentices learn their craft, offering suggestions and pieces of advice at the moment of need, perhaps guiding the racket or the chisel, but mostly watching and listening as the apprentice practices strengths and works through weaknesses.

Belenky and her colleagues suggest a less male, less sports-oriented metaphor for the nurturing teacher I try to be: the teacher as midwife.

> Midwife-teachers are the opposite of [what Freire calls] banker-teachers. While the bankers deposit knowledge in the learner's head, the midwives draw it out. They assist the students in giving birth to their own ideas, in making their own tacit knowledge explicit and elaborating it. (217)

Besides being pedagogically sound, thinking of ourselves as coaches or midwives clarifies the boundaries of responsibility. Abandoning the "filling the student with knowledge" model makes clear the limits of our role. Even the best coach can't make a winner out of someone who won't play. We can motivate, cajole, model, instruct, develop or reduce competition, but for the student to improve, he or she has to swing the racket or bang the hammer. And we shouldn't punish ourselves if, for whatever reasons, the student refuses to do so.

The master-apprentice outlook puts the spotlight where it belongs—not on the teacher nor, really, on the student, but on the act of writing itself. It's worth mentioning this way of defining ourselves on the first day and reiterating it regularly. It's a switch for students used to thinking of themselves as blotters absorbing the teacher's knowledge, but both students and teachers gain from the coaching model in the long run.

We need to make students responsible

Perhaps my heading should be rephrased, "make students *aware* that they're responsible"; even a traditional, "professing" writing teacher can't be held accountable for most of what students do. I'm not advocating an abdication of the teacher's role; as I tell my students on the last day of class, I feel the writing of all my ex-students represents me, and I still cringe when I read an article by one of them and find a misplaced *it's*. Yet the more we can put responsibility on the shoulders of our students, the more we can reduce our own stress, and the closer our students will be to the goal of making their teachers and editors irrelevant, redundant.

Because I'm the grader, I would never pretend that my evaluation of a student's work doesn't matter, but from the first I try to get students involved in evaluating their own ideas and writing. They list possible topics, choose from the lists, find what's worth salvaging from their freewrites, select (sometimes with peers' help) from their lists of titles and leads. When they bring their papers to me in conference, I avoid the awful moment of judgment by getting them to talk about their paper first, usually by having them respond in advance to a list of feedback questions. Although occasionally students have a sincerely inflated idea of their paper's value (as opposed to putting up a brave front in order to con me), much more often they either have an accurate sense of their own strengths and weaknesses or totally deride what they have done.

Responding to student responses is much easier than responding to the paper itself. We can agree about specifics with the overly optimistic student ("Yeah, that detail is wonderful") while getting the student away from the notion that the draft is inviolable ("but I think you need to condense some other details so that this one stands out better"). Students who see their weaknesses accurately sometimes have an idea what to do about them, which allows us just to nod and send them on their way. Students who haven't a clue about what to do next put us in the enviable position of playing magician: "Why don't you put the paper aside for a moment and try listing all your reasons in a quick brainstorm? That might give you more to build on."

I'm not yet comfortable involving students directly in their final course grading. (Lynn Z. Bloom is. See her article, "Why I (Used to) Hate to Give Grades.") But as I mentioned in the previous chapter, I do have students analyze themselves as writers at the end of the semester. They learn about themselves—especially about their strengths, which I insist they focus on—and I learn something about how their work in the course fits into their writing history. Detailing what they know about writing gives students a different perspective on their work—one more like a teacher's—and usually teaches them more than any other work they do in the course.

Though it can be difficult for teachers to let go of the reins, the class as a whole can take over some of what we normally see as the teacher's responsibilities, leading students to take on a greater sense of ownership for class ideas. Instead of simply telling students how we define "good writing," for instance, we can let small groups and then the whole class jot down the elements important to them and group those elements into categories, connecting specifics ("makes the reader want to read on" and "has a good opening," for instance) and finding examples of generalizations (under "lively writing" for instance, we might list "use active verbs"). Students may take a couple of hours of class time to build a definition of good writing, but if they do it well and stay in charge, they feel some loyalty to the results and are less likely to gripe that they're writing for the teacher.

Students can also start and lead discussions about readings and issues, taking the pressure off the teacher to come up with the brilliant insight, the meaning, the answer. I often have students write briefly, then discuss in turn what they wrote. Of course, using such a method may mean that the teacher needs to let go of specific goals for the discussion or hope that students bring up the "right" points. But rather than work toward the *truth* about an issue or a reading, the teacher can be happy reaching other goals—100 percent participation, for instance, or full development of student interests in a subject.

We should forget about model writers

Many of us harbor images of ideal writers or writing. We may not say we want our students to be Hemingways, but we trumpet the merits of the short declarative sentence. Or, with Henry James in the back of our minds, we practice sentence combining until our embeddings have embeddings. Or, more commonly, we think back to what we needed or what helped us at crucial stages in our development as writers and try to provide our students with what would have worked for us.

As long as we don't insist on the superiority of one method or style, such approaches won't harm students, but they're unlikely to help much, either, because all of them set goals that have nothing to do with the individual student and that student's writing. Instead of taking on the weight of making our students into young John McPhees or Toni Morrisons, we'll be more successful, and less stressed, if we try to get out of students' way and let them be themselves.

The history of American literature conveys the clear message that no one style is best. The two most admired poets of the American nineteenth century—Dickinson and Whitman—couldn't be more different stylistically. And while Hemingway fans argue his style defined the twentieth century's, advocates of the radically different styles of Faulkner and Nabokov can wrestle that issue to a draw. English teachers should be especially wary of using their younger selves as models since proto-writers and proto-English teachers constitute the exceptions rather than the rule. We had "natural" good grammar; we liked to read even when we didn't have to; some of us even liked to write. Many teachers of first-year English see such a student once a year, at best.

If we needed any more reasons to be leery of pushing students towards a universal ideal, multiculturalists eagerly point out that notions of good writing are culturally determined. Much of the rest of the world views the American stylistic goals of clarity and coherence, with specifics building a case for a generalization, as the equivalent of fast-food, lacking the beauty and multiple meanings of less direct approaches (see Li).

What's the alternative to setting our sights on an ideal? To accept student writers where they are and help them improve. As Noddings says, "I begin, as nearly as I can, with the view from [the student's] eyes" (15). I would seldom want to guess what a student's style or voice ultimately should or will be like, but I can almost always see ways in which the paper of the moment can be improved. A student whose sentences run on endlessly, incomprehensibly, needs help breaking them into manageable units. Another who writes short, repetitive sentences needs to learn sentence combining techniques.

If our goal is "better," not "elegant," we're less likely to be disappointed and more likely to engage the student in defining and reaching that goal. And if we don't set our sights on one kind of style, we will help our students unravel the mystery of voice.

Many student writers worry that if they eliminate the purple flourishes of their own prose, the convoluted sentence structures they employ to avoid writing another subject-verb-object sentence, their writing will sound like everyone else's. Such worries seem legitimate, but ironically the more writers pare their prose and clean the dross from its surface, the more different and original the prose appears, the more it reflects the individuality of a unique mind. Sometimes I give my class sentences to revise: "Pursuant to the recent memorandum issued August 9, 1999, because of petroleum exigencies, it is incumbent upon us all to endeavor to make maximal utilization of telephonic communication in lieu of personal visitation." One student might come up with: "Call, don't visit"; another, "Use the telephone instead of the car"; another, "Because of the gas crunch, please reduce your use of company cars." We can help students see that sometimes they hide behind a style or a vocabulary. They'll develop a personal voice not so much by adding adjectives and metaphors as by stepping forth from behind the verbiage.

Our ability to pursue seventy-five different writing improvement plans each semester may some day be valued as the impressive skill that it is; in "The Concept of a Knowledge Base," Robert Donmoyer identifies "an emerging

consensus" that such "flexibility to respond appropriately to the idiosyncra-
cies of particular students and particular classrooms" is one of a teacher's
most valued skills (98).

We need to be fair, not objective

This is one of Don Murray's maxims that I most frequently invoke. For at least
thirty years, since New Journalism began making its influence felt, journalists
on the cutting edge have admitted that objectivity is a mirage, something
not even a photograph can achieve. Yet like the ideal American writing style,
"objectivity" hovers over English classes, casting a shadow on everything we
do. Teachers and writers alike feel judged and found wanting by the universal
standard of objectivity; we know neither we nor our students can reach it, but
we feel guilty if we don't urge them to try.

Fairness, on the other hand, is openly, admittedly, subjective and situa-
tional. Yet it is also achievable, and working towards it provides good exercise in moral judgment. If I were to try to be objective about a paper arguing
against gun control, I would have to admit defeat, recuse myself from the
bench. But while admitting my subjectivity, I think I can be fair about it. The
pretense of objectivity strives to remove the issue of moral judgment. "Fairness" accepts the observer's humanity and challenges the observer to use his
or her best judgment to achieve a fair and humane solution.

We shouldn't try to go it alone

An active composition community can help ease the individual teacher's
overwhelming sense of responsibility. Just knowing that other people face the
same crises, the same doubts, the same annoying student complaints, relieves
us of the sense that "I must be doing something wrong." Hearing in a staff
meeting on the first sunny spring day, "Boy, aren't they hard to keep on task?"
can put to rest a whole chorus of inner blaming voices.

We stress less if we remember that twenty or thirty colleagues probably
have solutions to the seemingly insoluble student problem of the moment. I
now have enough ideas stored away to double or triple the length of any composition course, but when I first got started, I was hungry for activities that
would eat up the hours in a productive way, and my colleagues never let me
down, introducing me to some of the activities that make up the last chapter
of this book. Old-timers need to let newcomers know that such borrowing is
OK, common, part of the game.

We also need to spread the sense of responsibility for keeping ourselves
sane, keeping our own chins up. Alone, we're inevitably going to doubt the
value of what we do, become convinced that we don't deserve the respect we're

not getting. But when I've had a bad day, often my office neighbor has had a good one, or has recently talked to one of my ex-students who praised me or my class.

As composition instructors have gradually recognized how much we share with other writing teachers around the country, individual instructors and formerly isolated writing staffs have begun connecting through the proliferation of composition journals and conferences, the growth of composition listserves such as ECOMP-L, and the development of the National Writers Union (<http://www.nwu.org/nwu/>) and the National Adjunct Faculty Guild (which now offers a magazine, books, a newsletter, a dossier service, and even health insurance at <http://www.sai.com/adjunct/NAFGS.html>). Our connections can now take place through a myriad of channels and at any distance.

Connections with colleagues can be the difference between burning out and enjoying ourselves. A tight, congenial composition staff can act as one large diverse-but-unified consciousness, able to provide almost anything the individual needs. Together we figure out how to respond to the new gen. ed. requirements or what to do about the rash of harassing male students. We exchange tips on books, articles, difficult or outstanding students.

Like students lonely with their own "wrong" interpretations, some composition instructors who haven't connected with their peers worry that only they feel so undervalued and conflicted and isolated. They don't last long unless they can start borrowing from their cohorts not just good classroom techniques but good techniques for survival: how to cope, how to share, what to borrow.

Only colleagues can tell me how to cut corners and which ones to cut. Only they fully appreciate my favorite punctuation handout. When I'm depressed about a class, they describe the semester they taught the same class morning and afternoon: what failed in one succeeded in the other. They relate debacles even worse than the one I just survived. The camaraderie that develops among composition instructors becomes for some a chief allure of the job: a mixture of the solidarity of fellow craftspeople, the cohesion of facing a common enemy, and the gallows humor of people who have been treated like rats and feel the ship wallowing beneath them.

I've learned particularly from the different coping mechanisms of people I've worked with. Some find dignity in reading *CCC* and going to CCCC, giving papers, engaging in scholarly debate, as though they had a "real" composition job and a real future in the discipline. Others cope by minimizing the psychological importance of teaching in their life. They still do a good job—often because the other half of their life is creative and nourishes their teaching—but they're almost immune to ego damage resulting from insults to the profession. Still others insist on their status as writers-who-teach, actively developing their writing and their reputation, sometimes building a sense of superiority to professors-who-teach-writing, who know writing only from books and theories.

As a writing director, Don Murray was particularly effective at helping composition instructors feel that the weight of the job could be spread across many shoulders. The community of writers that worked with Don lived the motto (from Yvor Winters, I believe): "A victory for one writer [or writing teacher] is a victory for all."

Composition instructors may not have much in the eyes of the university and the world, but we've got numbers and a built-in sense of empathy. We'd be crazy not to use them.

8

Reduce Our Time Investment

It's 5:45 on a Thursday. It's dark outside, and the evening classes haven't yet begun. On the first floor, lights glow in only two rooms, where professors rattle away on keyboards and make occasional phone calls. On the third floor, though, there's a constant hum of conversation, as three composition instructors stretch their days to try to accommodate all their students. A student leaves one of the offices and the instructor gets up, stretches, looks at the long list on her door, sighs, and settles back into her chair to wait for the next (now late) student.

Teaching writing well takes time. Generally speaking, the more time we devote to an individual student's writing, the more that writing improves. This relationship is problematic in two ways for composition instructors. For one thing, few people outside the composition world realize how much time paper reading and student writing conferences take; they can't fathom how poorly class hours represent the amount of work that composition teachers actually do. The more vexing issue for composition instructors trying to find a way to do their job well and have a life is that cutting our time investment seems inevitably to hurt students. We're caught in an untenable position.

Although I have some suggestions of ways to reduce the total time spent on writing courses without shortchanging students, writing this chapter made me uncomfortable because I'm not happy withholding anything from students that I think might help them improve. The decisions discussed in this chapter are not easy. We have to face the unpleasant reality that our institutions pay us for a tiny percentage of the work we do, and instead of taking up

76

all the slack ourselves, shortchanging ourselves and our families and eventually burning out and quitting, we need to come closer to giving our students what the institution pays for. We can do that and still provide them with a unique and valuable experience.

Papers and Homework

For many of us, reading and responding to student papers defines our teaching experience. The symbol of our lives is The Stack: homework, in-class writing assignments, journals, drafts of every stripe and polish, writing for every purpose and audience. Although when friends find us drowning in a sea of paper, we're most likely to explain bravely, "That's my job," we can limit the time we spend awash in that sea without seriously compromising our pedagogical effectiveness. Instructors who haven't yet evolved their own way to read papers efficiently may find that the most productive reading they can do is in the extensive literature on handling paperwork. Knoblauch and Brannon's study established, almost twenty years ago, the extent and pointlessness of paper-marking overkill. At about the same time, the NCTE threw out its life ring, *How to Handle the Paper Load* (Stanford). Drawing on these studies and others, Hairston presents common-sense alternatives to "The Conventional Wisdom about Paper Grading" in her article "On Not Being a Composition Slave" (117).

Here I list just a few of the methods and attitudes that have helped me spend less time on student papers. In Chapter 10, I continue the discussion with an eye towards reducing teachers' guilt and worry.

We don't, after all, have to read everything students write; they can get response and validation in other ways. Students feel relieved, free, if we say ahead of time that we're not going to collect certain assignments or in-class writing. Some enjoy exchanging papers with one other person or with a group. Others like to read their work aloud, knowing that few people criticize a public reader. We can ask them to build a portfolio to turn in at the end of the course or to write a letter about what they've been learning from their in-class writing.

We can also spend a lot less time marking up papers. It took me years to minimize my marginalia on final drafts. Yet who does more than look at the grade and read the final comment? Who's going to revise a final paper? We usually know when a student is committed enough to work beyond the grade. For everyone else, less is more.

Although spending less time on student papers makes many of us feel guilty, it can also buffer us against the despair of feeling ineffectual. When we spend hours carefully reading, responding to, and talking to a student about a paper, and then the revision or even just the individual paragraph doesn't improve, we tend to question the value of everything we do. When we focus more of our attention on student writers who actively seek it, our work produces results, our egos are less threatened.

Readings

Cutting down on reading, too, is a difficult professional decision. Ideally, students should read as much as they can possibly fit into their schedules. Yet if they do, we do too, it seems, and assigning hundreds of pages of reading means the assigner has less time for anything but schoolwork.

We can, in fact, cut down on our reading time without reducing our students'. I assign my students to find a nonfiction author who appeals to them and read extensively from that author's work, then do a number of different assignments on the author, including bringing in a piece of the author's work for all to read and discuss. They immerse themselves enough to get a sense of style, they bask in being the expert, and I read only the small portion that the class reads. Having students extensively research a subject of their choosing can have similar benefits.

We can also make more use of what we *have* to read—student papers. Don Murray says that the text of a writing class should be the students' writing, and while there are benefits to reading professional pieces (Murray, after all, has his own selection of professional writing, *Read to Learn*), I think most of us would do well to pay more attention to Murray's advice. Most of the points we'd want to make with professional writing we can make with our class papers, and usually students care more about their peers' efforts than they do about some expert's. (See Tobin's section "Student-Authored Textbooks," 121–127.) We don't even need to use whole papers. I've had good luck assembling a collection of leads or of exemplary passages that I call "gems," one from each class member, and having the class generalize a theory of successful leads or of good writing by looking at the class samples and figuring out why some work particularly well.

It's good to remind ourselves that we're not teaching literature classes. Many people become composition teachers because they go to English graduate school to pursue a love of reading and then find that teaching composition allows literature lovers to eat. But I cringe when I hear new teaching assistants rattle off their reading list, the favorite books they've waited so long to tell others about. When I assign more reading than I can discuss in class, I worry that my students may become cynical and selective about all my assignments. We need to challenge the reasons for and the value of all the reading we assign.

Conferences

I focus much of this chapter on writing conferences with students because they're so effective yet so time-consuming. I realize that many composition instructors, saddled with four or five courses each semester, already see conferences as a luxury. For those people, my message is that conferences are possible even under the worst conditions. Students need them. Weekly conferences yield the best student portfolios, create the most intense relationships, and maximize motivation and student commitment to writing. At UNH, when Don Murray's influence was strongest, instructors conferred with all their students almost every week; someone teaching three sections of Freshman English spent fifteen to twenty hours a week talking individually to students. Marathon conference sessions left us plenty punchy at the end of the day, but it was a satisfying punchiness. We developed warm, comfortable relationships with students and watched the drafts get better week by week. I still think weekly conferences are the standard by which writing courses should be judged.

I'm sure that some people at UNH and elsewhere still meet students weekly, but most composition instructors, caught between a workload that grows and a paycheck that doesn't, have to compromise and find ways to reduce the burden of conferences. A relatively easy step is to move to biweekly conferences, with peer groups meeting in the "off" weeks. My students seem to have a positive experience in the groups about three-quarters of the time: "I really liked having another audience to write to"; "At first it was hard for me to criticize someone else's paper, but I think I learned to say some things that were useful."

When I see papers only every two or three weeks, they tend not to get as good by the end of the semester as they would have if we had had weekly meetings. But that may well be less important than students' discovering that they can improve their writing on their own and with the help of peers.

Peer writing groups require training and some kind of accountability; listening to students trying to help each other can make us appreciate our own expertise at such conversations. I don't feel I've yet evolved the perfect peer group handout, but I like to give them something like the one in Figure 8–1 so I can keep referring them back to what they're supposed to be doing.

Group conferences—having two, three, or four people meet at the same time with the instructor—can also save the instructor time. The conference

You can organize and write your response in any way you like, but somewhere in your response try to do the following. Be specific whenever possible. Enjoy the experience of communicating about something that matters to someone who cares.

1. Write a narrative or summary of your impressions of the piece. What happens in this paper? What is it trying to do? What are your general impressions of the voice of the piece and the character of the author? At this point don't make any judgments or even try to discern a point. You might think of this as the equivalent of an active listener's response: "What I hear you saying is . . . " I often start off my response to a poem with something like "My reading of this is. . . ." (For example, a possible beginning of a narrative of one reader's impressions of Scott Sanders's "The Inheritance of Tools" would be: "In the first paragraph you connect pain, tools, and your father right away. I thought maybe the paper was going to be about anger at your father. But then in the next couple of paragraphs, you're very respectful to him. . . .")

I may have offered too many alternatives in that paragraph. Choose one that makes sense to you and run with it.

2. Discuss how the piece connects to your life. Does it raise any questions that might be interesting for you to pursue or offer any answers to your own questions?

3. Provide your own answer to the "So what?" question. What is the paper's point, purpose, reason for being? What takes it beyond being *just* an exercise or *just* an anecdote or *just* a description? Don't give up easily on this question. If at first you see no point, dig, stretch, speculate. Your "wild guess" tells the author a lot about the impression the piece is making.

4. What works? What makes you laugh or surprises you or provides you with useful information? What is concise or insightful, well-phrased or well-thought? What grabs you or moves you or surprises you or makes you stop to think? Don't skimp on this one; it may be the most important. Writers revise and grow by building on their strengths.

Figure 8–1. *Feedback Guidelines and Questions*

5. What might the author add or expand in order to answer questions that the paper has raised? What do you need to hear more about?

6. What sections seem less purposeful than others? Be careful how you phrase this. Just because you don't see the point in a paragraph doesn't mean that the paragraph is "pointless." Saying honestly "I don't get it" gives a clear but not a harsh message to the author.

7. What confused you? What parts did you have to read twice? Don't be satisfied with saying "Oh, I figured it out." If you stumbled on a spot, other readers will too, and the author needs to know that.

8. (Optional and not usually recommended.) Make specific suggestions about changes—offer an alternative title or phrase, or perhaps a source the author might consult. Probably the best way to handle this step is to make notes for yourself about specific things on a draft that you might want to change, then when you get together, ask the author how much detailed critique she or he wants to hear, and what kinds of comments would be most helpful.

resembles an in-class group meeting, but with the addition of the watchful eye (or guiding hand) of the teacher. One student author leads off by asking the group for feedback about particular issues, and students usually try to imitate the workshop behaviors they've learned in class. Student writers often pay more attention to a consensus of their peers than to the teacher, and meeting with a small group may increase students' motivation and therefore lead them to put more work into a paper.

I've tried group conferences but wasn't happy with them for two perhaps overly personal reasons: I miss the intimate one-on-one connection, and I get frustrated when peers' voices overrule me. No doubt sometimes peers' ideas are more helpful than mine, but I have enough professional pride to think I can identify strengths, diagnose problems, and suggest solutions better than they can, and I don't want to be in competition with them. So while many good teachers find group conferences an effective compromise measure, for my personality they're not an attractive option.

Particularly busy composition instructors can experiment with the kinds of in-class conferences widely used in elementary and secondary schools (see, for instance, Rief [122] and Atwell [Chapter 5]). While the rest of the class writes or works in small groups, individual students meet with the teacher in a quiet corner one by one, usually for less than five minutes. The success of such a system depends on students' readiness; we need to train them to be prepared with a question or two that they need answered. Just-in-time miniconferences may well become the dominant type, even in college seminars; like grammar minilessons (see Weaver, 171), they're efficient and probably effective. But I think I will always retain my leisurely quarter-hour chats at the beginning of the semester when students and I connect the details of our lives and bond against the students' writing demons.

I feel particularly ambivalent about reducing or eliminating required conferences altogether and doing what most professors do—allow students to drop in or sign up for office hours if they want to. Such an approach—which I assume approximates a norm for composition instructors nationwide—teaches students lessons about using resources wisely, planning ahead, figuring out when feedback most benefits them. Students who want frequent meetings with the teacher can get them. Students who experiment consciously with their writing process and with getting feedback in different ways and at different times can probably learn as much from "sign-up" conferences as from scheduled weekly ones. Those who don't take advantage of conference time often suffer as a result, though they *may* learn something from their loss, and they *may* make more use of the services of a reader next time they have the opportunity.

Philosophically, I'd rather give students the option to come to conference and let them figure out whether it's worth their while. But realistically, I know that without a little arm twisting, most students will cut corners, procrastinate, do mediocre work, and not get as much out of the course as they could.

Manipulating the time we spend in conference is a particularly tricky issue because our feelings about conferences are so complex. On the one hand, if we let students choose when to confer, we spend less time in the office, which should be a gain. But when only half the class comes to talk with me about an assignment, I feel both somewhat insulted and as though I'm not doing my job. I'm invested in seeing one-on-one time with me as irreplaceable.

Disengaging our egos a bit from the effectiveness of conferences can help us reduce guilt about trimming conference time. After all, we want to help students become independent enough and trusting enough of peers so that we become unnecessary. We no doubt routinely overload them with feedback anyway. I have to admit that sometimes I cling to the extra conference time because without it I feel I don't get to know individual students as well. It seems ironic to admit that I spend all that time voluntarily, but it makes me feel less of a victim to recognize that I'm doing it at least partly for myself.

Without necessarily changing the frequency of conferences, we can make them more efficient, and therefore perhaps cut down on their length, in a number of ways. Conferring cold—reading the paper when the student brings it in and responding immediately—saves a lot of time over reading papers at home and then talking about them in conference. In a cold conference, I read the paper in five minutes or less and decide on the spot what I need to ask or say.

"So you feel that bombing Nagasaki was justified?"

"This description of your daughter in the hospital brings me to tears."

"This leaves me thinking about your anger, not the tobacco companies' guilt. Is that what you want?"

"I'm fascinated by what you said about your sense of responsibility, but I'm also confused."

Often a spontaneous reaction to two or three aspects of the paper helps the student more than a detailed, thought-out response, written or oral. I give my students the option of leaving me with drafts before the conference or bringing them in when they come to talk, so they have control over the kind of feedback they get. Anyone who has avoided cold conferences should try them. Doing them well takes practice, but it's a fascinating art. One second I'm thinking "What on earth am I going to say about this paper?" and the next second I'm saying something.

I manage always to have something to say because I usually get the student to start the discussion. I may ask for written feedback with every paper and start by reading that and responding to it. Or I may ask the student, "What surprised you?" "How did you write this?" or "Are you happy with how it turned out?" The student who says "This is the roughest thing I've ever shown anyone. I just want to know if the idea is worth pursuing" needs a very different response from one who says "I think this is about done. Did you see any grammar problems?" Both of them need a shorter, more limited and focused response than we would normally give if we just started writing comments about the paper. Making students responsible for directing our conversation is both pedagogically sound and a time-saver.

Many of us have trouble limiting our comments, whether we're saying them aloud or writing them in the margins or at the end. We have to keep reminding ourselves that most students can deal with only a couple of issues in a paper at a time, and giving them more is likely both to demoralize the student and to waste our time. Choosing two or three issues is often harder than filling a quick page with responses, but it's a valuable exercise for us and a favor to our students.

I choose my two or three things with a desire above all to engage the student in a discussion about the main meaning of the piece. Often I become a mirror reflecting to the writer the paper's many facets: "I first thought this was going to be about your mother-in-law's intolerance. But at the end you develop a sense of solidarity with her, which made me think that overcoming that intolerance was key for you. Your title, on the other hand, points to your husband's relationship with his mother as the center. Which of those should I have foremost in my mind when I get to the end?"

Of course I always choose something positive. Because my students almost always have a fair amount of control over their choice of topics, they usually care about their subjects, so even if they have no sense of focus and their sentence structure gives me a headache, I can always find something in which I'm sincerely interested.

"Do you think male doctors perform more episiotomies than female doctors?"

"How do the fisher*men* treat a woman out there with a fly rod?"

"You taught me a lot about why people go four-wheeling."

We can also choose from numerous alternatives to standard conferences and comments. I'm not sure that e-mail and other electronic communication save time, but they allow us to time shift and respond to students when it's most convenient. And we should never ignore the possibilities of quick before- or after-class confering. Sometimes the student who stays after and asks me to read her lead advances as much as the student who gets a full fifteen-minute conference of my attention.

I applaud composition instructors' versatility, the variety of our jobs, the many roles that we play. But we need to guard against thinking that we can be all things to all people. It's comforting but probably not realistic to imagine that every second we invest in our classes pays off, and that sense of our impressive efficacy breeds the guilt we feel when we trim our class preparation hours even slightly. It is possible to teach well with less time, but we may have to give up some ego involvement to do it.

9

Be Selfish—and Improve Our Teaching

Sue looks beat at the one o'clock staff meeting. She spent the weekend grading a set of papers and is keeping up her usual grueling conference schedule that always stretches an hour longer than planned because of her well-known determination to give each student what she or he needs. I know she's also been trying to finish a book about fiction writing before this week's deadline.

But it isn't any of those things, she confides quietly to the people around her. "When Katie got to the point of having to call somebody, the only somebody she could think of was me. So I was up for three hours last night talking to her, trying to get in touch with a counselor or her parents, calling her back every few minutes to convince her I hadn't forgotten about her. She seemed calmer this morning," Sue smiles weakly, "but I sure could use some sleep."

Selfish people don't usually end up as teachers, especially not composition teachers, particularly not nontenure-track composition teachers being paid $1200 per course. The money's bad, the tangible benefits few; we have, it would seem, every reason to loaf, to make school a low priority. Yet we all want to do a good job, and that usually means continuing to sacrifice ourselves, putting the student first. Judy Wells' Part-Time Teacher "wonders whether she should call in the California Self-Esteem Task Force and ask them what is wrong" (3).

Because of these tendencies, most composition teachers need to guard against being too self-sacrificing. Veterans like Sue know how to give up a night's sleep for a student, do their work the next day, still meet the deadline for their own writing, and measure their worth in human rather than monetary terms. But slipping into the martyr or victim mentality almost inevitably

85

leads to burnout, a career crisis, and one more good teacher quitting to get an M.B.A. and hunt the elusive cash cow. To survive in this profession, we need consciously to do things for ourselves—things that we enjoy, things that help us grow, things that make all the sacrifices seem worthwhile. Luckily, many such things actually improve our effectiveness as teachers.

Share Our Writing

Most of us keep teaching for the chance to stand in front of a roomful of people and, whenever we want, share our stories, our opinions, our writing, revel in showing off and being creative. The composition classroom is not always a welcoming, accepting place, but when the class goes well, we emerge nurtured, rewarded. We need that stage, that chance to control and get the last word. When I jog, drive, take a shower during the school year, I almost invariably talk to my class in my head, knowing that at least some of them will listen to my take on the latest presidential blunder, laugh at my jokes, get excited by my newest insight about writing.

Students often come up after the first class of the semester and say, with evident surprise and pleasure, "I've never seen a teacher write on the board before." I usually talk to them about pedagogy, not personal gratification, but I'm always thinking, "All those other English teachers—they don't know what they're missing."

Though most of what I write in class never even makes it onto disk, I delight in producing off-the-wall ideas, making surprising connections, digging up long-lost details, watching tangents turn into possible topics. Even when I tell students not to try to read my scribbles but concentrate on their own, they're eager to see what I wrote, impressed that I can do it in public and produce something interesting in three minutes, and often inspired to do something similar. I write, read, create, analyze, connect, teach, get facial if not verbal feedback all at virtually the same moment. Such times have an alluring immediacy, an intensity I wouldn't trade for many experiences I know. Gradually developing the confidence that I could do such "work" any time, anywhere, has constituted the greatest part of what I might term "professional growth," although that growth only indirectly affects publications, conference presentations, and other measures of professional advancement.

Writing in front of a class the first time probably made my heart pound, although I don't remember that moment. Today, when I finish explaining freewriting to students and turn to the board to start scribbling myself, I still get a dose of adrenaline, a sense of preparing to dive into cold water on a hot day. But I'll take the energy and the dive every time. When I'm between semesters, looking ahead to the next one, I get myself psyched for yet another opening day by thinking about standing before them and messing up a freshly cleaned blackboard.

As I see it, writing in front of the class is a can't-lose situation, an opportunity few others can match. I'm not an exhibitionist; when I'm skiing, writing on a computer, or playing music, I hate having an audience. But like, I assume, almost everyone, I enjoy being the center of attention, having students strain to follow my many-engined train of thought and laugh at my details and the things I say to myself in my writing. The sense that no one will ever read what we're writing, that it doesn't really matter, paralyzes many writers, so the opposite feeling, that people will be reading even the most banal, tawdry of our thoughts liberates us. It provides me with the energy to produce more and better work in a quick five-minute spurt of class activity than an hour at my computer often yields. And of course if our chalky "garbage drill" produces nothing but garbage, the eraser is always at hand, and we haven't wasted any of our precious home writing time.

I get a similar charge explicating my writing to make a pedagogical point. I could make the same point with hypothetical examples, but when I show students a train of thought in my freewriting and have them follow the tangent to the new and exciting idea, or when I demonstrate how different titles point to very different papers on the same subject, my examples are not only real, convincing, and timely, but because they're mine, saturated with my own images and associations, I can throw in other pedagogical points, make little stabs at humor, or sprinkle politics throughout the demonstration without losing sight of my point.

My instant in-class writing is uneven: sometimes I'm pleased with a line, an image, a juxtaposition of words; sometimes my sentences make me groan. But again, I can't lose. If I produce something flashy, I awe the students and feel like Houdini. If I produce schlock, I can say so, point out the ideas worth salvaging, and reiterate that we need to produce lots of garbage in order to come up with a gem or two. I don't, of course, know what goes through students' minds, what kind of judgments they make, but usually they're prepared to be impressed with what I do, and I know that they're impressed that I do it. Writing in public seems as difficult to them as playing guitar in public looks to me.

Writing in front of our students is a pedagogical tool without peer. It establishes, first, that writing—even when it produces junk—is important enough for this expert, this "professor" to spend class time on. My demonstrations of writing a variety of leads or turning a brainstorm into an outline also help make those processes much more tangible and comprehensible.

Students feel more comfortable with their own jerky, idiosyncratic writing processes when they see me speed along for a moment, stop, frown, ponder, laugh, speed again, stop in frustration.

We can also, of course, share our finished writing, choosing pertinent and helpful gems. I often read aloud a story I wrote about my grandfather because it allows me to explain, better than any other story can, the fuzzy line between fiction and nonfiction, the making of a focused story out of a memory, the importance of a recursive writing process and of good readers. I always get rewarded: by the end of the reading, two or three students have tears in their eyes, at least that many have been inspired to write their own pieces about important people in their lives getting old, and even students who set out to resist me have grudgingly admitted that I can do it. I can no longer say whether personal self-gratification or effective pedagogy leads me to keep reading the story; the two intertwine perfectly.

Teach Our Passion

Everyone knows what we should teach: while society doesn't value our work enough to pay us a living wage, many people are not shy about suggesting what we should or should not do in class. We need to provide multicultural diversity or make our students culturally literate, accept students' own language or enforce the language's high standards, prepare students to write lab reports or executive summaries, act as role models or loco parents or the one friendly human face in the anonymous megaversity.

As a result of persistent pressures to act in certain ways and teach certain things, many of us become hesitant to do what we really want to do, to bring our passions into the classroom. "We have no right to inflict ourselves on students," we worry. "We'd better stick to what studies have shown interests students, pleases parents, or satisfies 'content' professors."

But if we leave our own passion at the classroom door, so will our students, and while some passions—for guns or teenage lovers, for instance—clearly don't belong in class, integrating our interests into our courses keeps us and our students excited.

Over the years, my colleagues have successfully integrated into their classes photography, film, plays, sports, poetry, quilts, hypertext, particular authors, particular goals (self-discovery, surprise), particular sources of inspiration (dreams). I've taught a literature class on "novels on the fringes of the genre" and writing classes focused on the sixties and on the topic "questioning authority." Though some English departments may frown on writing teachers straying beyond the prescribed "grammar etc." content, many if not most courses offered by literature faculty either overtly or covertly focus on the professor's passion. That is, after all, one of the professor's jobs: to do enough work in an area to become an expert in it and pass that expertise on to students. Some people just have an easier time accepting "historical responses to Shakespeare" as a passion than science fiction or popular culture or the history of the essay.

As you've no doubt guessed, music is my main classroom passion. I play a selection at the beginning of virtually every class period. The music energizes some students, provides others with a welcome cover for conversations, seriously engages a few, and gives me a chance to make points about writing and literature in a unique and memorable way.

I usually start with a need—I need to demonstrate effective leads or to explain "unreliable narrator" or to talk about the difficulties of an all-white audience discussing African American writing or to present a brief history of, in Buffy Sainte-Marie's words, "the genocide basic to this country's birth." Then I turn to my music collection, which started in 1960 with the purchase of Dicky Lee's "The Tale of Patches and Other Tragic Love Songs" and grows virtually every day. As much as I may try to broaden my musical library, it clearly reflects my race, gender, age, and predilections, and when we talk about things like the canon or racism, those reflections of my bias become subjects for class inquiry: Have you noticed that I've only played one woman musician in the first eight classes? Does that bother you? Should I bring affirmative action to my music playing?

As I discuss elsewhere in this book, music connects me with my students, allows us to communicate in important and substantive ways, gives me a whole bag of tools for defining concepts, generating interest, unlocking minds. A part of almost everyone's life, music is a natural interest to exploit, but all the subjects I listed earlier—plus such obvious others as television, advertising, history, mythology, or fashion—could be equally successful if used creatively and critically. I can't say for sure whether students respond because it's my passion, because of the intellectual value of the music I play, or just because they enjoy having music in class, but they almost always praise music above everything else in my student evaluations.

Almost everyone who teaches composition harbors a passion for some kind of reading, and it's silly and self-defeating to pass over those favorites when putting together a syllabus. Of course we have to be careful about overdoing it or assuming that students resemble younger versions of ourselves; I wrote part of my dissertation on James Fenimore Cooper, but I haven't yet found the right class in which to teach one of his novels. We also need to avoid the trap that many of our teachers fell into, teaching the same books for decades, rigidly tied to a unique canon. We have to keep reading and teaching new books, expanding our own list of favorites, listening to students' enthusiasm and adding Dave Barry, Robert Fulghum, or Bailey White to our reading packet.

Despite all these cautions, however, enthusiasm should be a prerequisite for almost all the books we teach. Teaching a book because it fits perfectly or is on everyone's "classic" list may sound great when we're planning the course, but if it's not on our list, will we have the energy to convince students to give it a chance? A teacher's enthusiasm for a book is not sufficient to make students like it, but it may well be necessary.

Connect

It's impossible not to make connections while teaching, but like active reading, active connecting can pay off for us in many ways. Sometimes it's too easy for me to hide in my instructor's hovel, focus my conferences on papers, and never see my students in broader social contexts or meet the people with offices around the corner. But when I consciously take the time to go out to lunch with my colleagues, chat with new grad students down the hall, spend a few extra minutes with my students going beyond the paper, I feel better about the whole experience of teaching.

Only the community of writing instructors fully values our expertise and experience, so we turn to that community to find affirmation and the energy to face another twenty conferences. It's therapeutic to share with other instructors stories about how the department chair doesn't acknowledge us in the hall or how the benefits office claims we're neither faculty nor staff. As I describe in Chapter 7, the sharing of exercises, good readings, and student-handling tips, the sense of a support group that intimately knows what brings us down and can almost always suggest a way back up, the feeling of fitting into a group of intelligent, committed, talented people—these aspects of connection with colleagues keep composition instructors sane and help build respect for ourselves and our jobs. They also, of course, make us better teachers, since they bring ten or twenty or forty minds to bear on the day's student crisis, and they provide an inexhaustible supply of ideas for today's class.

The benefits to us of developing relationships with students that go beyond the paper may not be as obvious, but they're just as real and just as valuable. Since music often provides my first and most important bridge to students, it's not surprising that students have given me a lot musically. Like many people of my generation, I was for a while in danger of becoming a musical dinosaur, listening only to music that came out before I graduated from college, before production and marketing took over. When punk and new wave began evolving, I treated them as media bad jokes. But my students rescued me. Lana insisted that despite his ripoff name, Elvis Costello deserved a spot in the songwriter pantheon with Dylan and Lennon, and though I didn't pay attention until she had left my class, I eventually discovered she was right. Tom fed me tapes of X and the Sex Pistols until I began appreciating punk. BJ helped me over my prejudice against synthesized music by lending me a Nine Inch Nails CD. Ten years after the event, Karen helped me recognize Patti Smith's emergence as the biggest American rock news of the 1970s.

Because I'm easily persuaded to listen to new music, often I am won over by simple enthusiasm or by the student's taking the time to lend me a tape or CD. In other subjects, connections develop naturally around a paper. Roger helped me understand male hair dying by writing—and revising over and over—a paper about how and why he turned himself purple or green as a kid when he needed a change, something new in his life, a different outlook, motivations that would have led others to drugs or sexual experimentation or violent acting out. I still can't really imagine putting a metal ring through my lip or a bar through my tongue, but student papers have helped me see into the paradox of conformity/nonconformity and appreciate that when the conversation lags, you can always stick out your tongue. And did you know that the scarring produced by piercing a nipple makes it MORE sensitive?

Papers help me see into situations I'll probably never live through myself. Divorce has never affected my life, but I need to know about something so common and traumatic in our culture, and scores of papers have helped me understand the anger, damage, and occasional rebirth of the participants. By going beyond the predictable and surprising themselves, some writers give me insights that even most participants never reach. Pete, for instance, provided a window into postdivorce relational changes by focusing on the new relationship that developed between Pete and his father after Pete's mother left: his father became more human and Pete himself had to grow into and accept changes that he was not happy about. Similarly, while I'm quite sure I'll never go on a Mormon mission, and I used to consider people who did as alien to me as crayfish, having read some papers on it, I now realize that while some *are* alien, driven by a desire to cram their retooled Christianity down the throats of anyone who opens the door to them, many go for the most normal of reasons: because they're expected to, because Grampa promises a car upon their return, because they need a focus in life. I learn about similarity AND difference.

No matter what the subject, my desire to connect, my sincere interest in trying to understand the allure of fly-fishing or beauty pageants or Dungeons and Dragons, provides my students with an ideal audience. They get excited answering my questions in conference, and at least some can transfer that excitement into their papers. Again, the energy, the interest, the insights build with each contribution; the more selfishly students and I pursue our own needs, the more growth we can offer each other.

Of course I'm susceptible to the "do my work and get out of here" mentality, and in periods of extreme stress, that seems the only choice. But I recognize that when I exercise that option and don't make the effort to connect, when I don't put much of me into my work, it's my loss.

10

Handle Common Problems

My wife refers to the week after the last class as the week of sighs. I sit on the sofa with my gradebook and stack of papers, occasionally moving everything down to the floor to pop up and write a long final comment to a student, agonizing over how to be positive yet still justify the C−.

And I sigh. B− or C+? It might make the difference between keeping or losing a scholarship or athletic eligibility. Yet I can't reward him for poor attendance, mediocre work in his revision group, and papers that might have been As if he had left himself the time to do them justice.

What is fair? What is humane? Where are my standards?

I sigh.

Our job is seldom dull, in part because every day brings a new set of problems: Where do we get a VCR at the last minute for a student's presentation? How do we explain the difference between *a* and *the* to a foreign student? How do we convince a class full of would-be language elitists that *utilize* is not inherently superior to *use*? While such issues keep us alert, and we can't usefully prepare for many of them, some problems that composition teachers face occur often enough to be worth thinking through and arming for ahead of time. I've listed four here, with suggestions for solving them.

The sighs are softer than they used to be, the week shorter, serious misgivings less common.

Reading and Grading Papers

Some of the most depressing moments in the life of a composition instructor come at the end of an eight-hour day of classes and conferences when, instead of being able to leave the job at the office and settle down for Seinfeld reruns, the overworked instructor arrives home to a three-inch stack of papers that need to be returned the next day.

We can't avoid that pile entirely unless we substitute exams for papers or hire a grader. But we can make the job less onerous. In Chapter 8, I discussed some ideas and listed some resources that can help us limit the amount of time we spend on papers. The suggestions here reduce the worry and guilt associated with paper reading. I find that I need to keep reminding myself of them because, like many composition teachers, I have to battle an instinctive feeling that the more I sweat over and write on student papers, the more they get out of it, the better person I am. So this list is not of surprises but of reminders.

- **They're not like us.** As a student, I always felt grateful for long written comments and ripped off if my professors responded to my days of sweat and typing with only a few oral suggestions. But it's a mistake to think that our students feel the same way. Very few of them are fledgling serious writers, English-professors-to-be. They're used to thinking that more comments mean more problems. We need to open our eyes to how students really react, not teach to our own adolescent selves.

- **Less is often more.** Yes, I too have been outraged by one-word comments (especially when, on the most important paper I wrote in graduate school, the one word, along with an A, was *begrudged*). But I think we need to curb the instinct to fill the margin and to address in an end note every important aspect of the paper. A few marginal notations and two or three sentences at the end can convey what almost all students want to hear—that the material engaged the teacher, some of the ideas impressed. A few of our better students also want help with problems they're worried about—punctuation or leads or "flow." We can pinpoint such worries by having students respond first to drafts; then a targeted line or two on the final paper—"Good job with the semicolons!"—will mean more than paragraphs of other responses.

- **Slower is not better.** Like some of our students who doggedly reread the book before a history final, remembering almost nothing as their eyes plod over the pages, we often feel that we owe it to our students to read their final drafts word for word, even though we may have read essentially the same paper three or four times before. One of my colleagues says she grades a class's final papers in an hour: she knows the papers well by the end of the semester and just needs to skim them for improvements and to confirm her sense of the appropriate grade. I haven't yet become that efficient, but I have experimented with estimating students' grades before I even look at final portfolios, and those estimates are almost as accurate and fair as the grades I spend days of sweat and sighs to reach.

Like any good readers, we need to be ready to adjust our reading speed to the individual paper, not just lock into grading mode and cruise on autopilot all weekend. As the speed-reading experts insist, we actually get a *better* sense of the overall paper when we skim than when we plod. We're not doing the student any favors if we catch all the subtle stylistic changes but miss a fresh sense of the whole.

- **Know what we're reading for.** If we just need to come up with a midterm grade, a close reading of the first paragraph can often give us a good indication. If we're writing comments, we need, first, to respond to the student's concerns and second to focus on recurring important issues. Focused, active reading may take more energy, but it's considerably more efficient than mechanically reading word by word.

- **Respond only to those who want comments.** I used to write long, sincere final comments to every student, balancing the high and low points of the student's semester, setting out a path towards improvement, making sure that the last thing they heard from me was positive. Then, at the appointed hour for picking up papers, I would sit waiting while maybe half the class stopped in for their papers and comments, and I would go home with ten hours' worth of heartfelt comments that no one will ever look at. Now I tell students, "If you want comments, give me a stamped, self-addressed envelope." Students willing to invest thirty-three cents get comments; if they don't want them, I don't bother to write them. And I try to apply the same principal throughout the semester. I ask them for feedback directions and monitor their reactions often, though I'm sure I still err with too much rather than too little.

The Quiet Class

If you want to see a composition teacher turn into quivering jelly in a matter of minutes, convince everyone in class to remain silent despite the instructor's prompts and pleas. Like the student slights I mention in Chapter 2, a silent class calls into question our value, our efficacy. Is anyone listening?

In those moments of panic, remember, it's probably not our fault. Many English teachers were the kind of students who wouldn't shut up in class; some of our students just happen to be the opposite, and occasionally we end up with a handful of them. While I continue to think of quiet classes as an energy drag, I try not to see them as a defeat. Even when it seems the entire class has taken a vow of silence, some simple things are worth trying.

- **Wait.** We know that, we've seen the studies that say teachers don't even wait long enough for a student to take a breath, but it's hard to remember to wait when no one responds to our question in the seconds it takes us to mentally repeat "C'mon!" fifty times. Research about gender and communication patterns indicates that by giving only a few seconds for students to respond, many of us may have unconsciously favored and encouraged aggressive men at the expense of more thoughtful women (see Diller, Houston, Morgan, and Ayim, 52–53). It doesn't take much to alter the talking dynamic in a class— the most talkative student's absence, one silent person making a breakthrough, the teacher's asking an unusual question. Maybe if we wait just three more seconds . . .

- **Write.** Students asked to discuss a fine point of characterization in a short story may barely remember that they read the story some time last weekend. Giving students a few minutes to respond in writing to a question focuses their minds on English and on the subject of the moment and helps them think through their ideas about it. I will try to start a discussion without having them write first only if I can see them already bubbling with things to say about the topic.

- **Go around the circle.** Although it's a legitimate and effective way to end the silence, calling on people who aren't volunteering makes me nervous—I don't want to increase the anxiety level. I feel better if everyone is in the same boat. So after students have written on the subject, I often have them form a circle, and then we go around the circle, reading or paraphrasing what we wrote. Though obviously artificial, this approach has a lot of advantages. It doesn't traumatize; most students seem at worst resigned to taking their turn. If the conversation reaches a dead end, I just turn to the next person in the circle for a new thought. Once a few people have spoken, the conversation usually takes off. I almost never make it all the way around the circle.

- **Build community.** If I decide that class quietness is not just an annoyance for me but a serious problem for everyone, then provoking talk becomes top priority and getting the right answers or progressing through the syllabus becomes secondary.

I've had students interview and write about each other to get them to feel more at ease with their classmates, to practice interviewing, and to work on focusing, creating a profile of their classmates, not just listing facts. When "personal" ads became the new communication channel a few years ago, I had students write ads about themselves and about what they wanted in a revision group mate.

If I do nothing else to make students comfortable with each other, I have them introduce themselves with name, major, hometown, and something unique and memorable about themselves. (Mine range from "I collect ticks" to "I have an adopted daughter.") I encourage "Do you know so-and-so?" questions; they build valuable bonds that may grow. Sometimes it's even worth staging elaborate introduction games or bringing brownies and having a party during a class period.

I always feel a little guilty when I spend a day "just" helping students get comfortable with each other, but such time usually pays off in the quantity of discussion and the quality of group work for the rest of the semester.

- **Ask different questions.** Sometimes we just need to ask questions that don't have right answers about subjects that interest students. Early in the semester I often encourage students to trade horror stories about English classes of the past. Unfortunately, almost everyone has one and is eager for a chance to vent, and their stories can give me an opening to talk about my anxiety-reduction program and the things that I will and will not do. Even bringing up the latest campus controversy can break the habit of silence.

- **Change the approach.** Even teachers who try to create a student-centered classroom often end up being the hub of the wheel in any discussion. They question, wait, respond to the student's answer, ask another question. And somehow the discussion never gains momentum. Along with "wait!" we also may need to remember "shut up."

- **Experiment with small groups.** Any teacher who uses small groups knows that students who are silent, cowed, even hostile in class can become the life of the small group. That fact can simply be aggravating for someone trying to build a whole-class discussion, but it gives the teacher of a silent class a good fallback position: if they won't talk, break them up. The dynamics of small-group work could fill a book by themselves; here I'm just advocating constant experimentation and rejection of the thinking that one unsuccessful small-group activity means they just won't work in a particular class.

Whether to manipulate groups is a big issue. Usually I let groups form on their own, but if that results in the same few people talking,

I take a more active role. I've tried putting the three or four quietest people in a group; their first few minutes together can be excruciating, but then almost always at least one person breaks out of his or her shell. Sometimes friends work well together, or I use surveys or my knowledge of their writing interests to group people with some common bond.

Probably the most fail-safe way to get small groups talking is to leave the room. When I come back, I can usually hear the class from far down the hall. Most groups are talking about parties or sports, but it's a start.

- **Let them take over.** The "leave the room" solution has useful analogues in the class even if we stick around. Capable, articulate students sometimes stay silent because they see it as the teacher's role to make the class work; they've had thirteen years' practice at being passive spectators of the teacher's song-and-dance. But make those same students responsible for some aspect of class functioning, and things change. I have them write on the board, summarizing a paragraph in the day's reading or listing issues that they wish someone would research. Individuals or groups can begin each day's reading discussion or present their own personal Process Insights and Hangups. Or groups can take responsibility for talking about particular aspects of a reading—the theme, the organization, the lead and end, the use of supporting details—and stumble their way to an understanding.

The Painful Conference

Chapter 8 discusses ways to spend less time in conference, approaches that usually require considerable thought before the course begins. Here I'm primarily concerned with making difficult conferences less stressful, using approaches that we can start applying this afternoon.

Fortuitously, the steps that make conferences easier for us also usually make them more valuable for students. I prefer "cold" conferences—reading the paper as the student waits and responding immediately—because students like and get more from quick response (the paper itself is often hot off the printer), and when I respond well, I only have time to bring up one or two issues, pedagogically a much more sound approach than delivering the student the truckload of comments that I'm likely to come up with when I've got days to think about the paper. Besides, cold conferences force me not to take too much time with the paper, and they don't give me much chance to worry about what I'm going to say and how the student will react.

Yet the cold conference can't eliminate the awful feeling of getting to the end of a terrible draft, wondering What am I going to say about this? The best answer is almost always Don't *say* anything, *ask*.

"How do you feel about this?"

"What surprised you here?"

"Do you want to keep working on this?"

Often, though unfortunately not always, the student knows that it's a weak draft and will feel relieved to have a chance to admit it.

I try to have students write down answers to feedback questions before they come to conference: *What do you like about this paper? What surprised you? What's your answer to the "So what?" question? Where should the next revision go?* (See other suggestions in Figure 8-1.) Then I can respond to their responses rather than directly to the paper. Even without that kind of preparation, we can put the burden on students' shoulders, explaining, if necessary, that writing classes should help students become their own best editors, rendering the teacher irrelevant.

The most difficult and belligerent students—who have usually grown up thinking that the teacher has all the answers and feel outraged when the teacher doesn't produce those answers—won't take a question for an answer and will shoot back, "What do YOU think about it?" At such junctures, we're faced with two options. We can play the "No, you go first" game, or we can give an honest answer, which is usually my preferred route: "I think it's got some good ideas but it doesn't seem as though you worked on it much." If the outraged student rejects that assessment, I'm likely to get the kind of response I was looking for in the first place ("I worked harder on this than any paper I've written in college, and I think that section about my father is . . . "), and I can shift to affirming the student's positive sense of what works and collaborating with the student to figure out what gives the impression of carelessness.

Difficult Students

There's nothing more draining and debilitating than spending the last forty-five minutes of a day talking with—or, more typically, listening to—a whiner. "I think I deserved a better grade . . . my roommate's papers aren't nearly as good, but he's getting As . . . I put so much time into this revision, but it's just getting worse . . . everybody else I showed it to thought it was great." We can't escape such people, but we can limit the amount of whining we have to put up with.

- **Set firm ends to conferences.** The most insidious whiners figure out that I usually go back to the office to work after class on Friday afternoon, and they tag along and moan at me for an hour. Being in general a sympathetic soft touch, I used to fall prey to such time-eaters, and I'd go home late and disgruntled. Now, unless a whiner appears at the beginning of a three-hour conference stretch that no one else has signed up for, I'm ready with a good reason to call a halt: I have to pick up my kids, my next class is about to start, Janine is waiting out there. Many of us need to make a conscious effort not to play the martyr. For the truly obnoxious whiner, a little rudeness is not out of order: I start putting papers into my backpack and sometimes stand up and hold open the door. I keep waiting for someone to push me to quote the words Pogo used to escape being the guest of honor at a possum pie dinner: "Gotta hurry home—Left the chillun on the stove" (Kelly, 13).

- **Be blunt.** Most of us work so hard to reduce anxiety, be sensitive to our students' problems, truly listen to them, that we may be reluctant to voice some of the hard truths of writing:

  Almost all writers feel as though they're the world's slowest

  Don't revise because you feel you ought to, do it because you can see a way to improve your paper

  If your roommate is getting As for weak work, that's his loss

  I don't want to condescend to you by giving you good grades for work we both know could be better.

  I'm not sure self-pity is ever a useful writing attitude. And while it's true that the blunt truth may piss off the whiner and result in a poor evaluation, lending a sympathetic ear for an hour and raising the grade may earn you "too lenient" on the final evaluation.

- **Don't argue.** If someone gripes about a grade, I automatically say, "Leave me with your paper(s). I'll reread them tonight and get back to you tomorrow." Even if I'm almost positive the grade will stand, I take another look because that move deflates the student's anger, seems rational and fair to even the most aggrieved, usually offers more than they've hoped for, and gets me out of the office and a difficult situation most quickly. I know that some students argue grades all the way to court these days, but I've never had a student continue to gripe after I had reconsidered.

- **Enlist on their side.** A whine quickly runs out of steam if we remove ourselves as the target, the ones responsible for all the woes. Too much work? I agree, but that's what the department demands. Afraid your revision is going nowhere? Let's look at the paper; I'm sure I can find some things that definitely need revision. Writer's block got you? Lower your standards, freewrite, talk it out. Grade too low? I was upset about it too; I don't know where all those comma splices came from.

- **Reread their resistance.** Robert Brooke argues that much student resistance, defiance, and off-task behavior is more related to the class activity than we might guess and is important for helping students create a sense of identity. In fact, some of the behaviors we find most annoying may show that students are following our example, acting on our principles, moving from a "contained" form of underlife to a "disruptive" form, a term that Brooke uses with approval.

11

Survive . . . and Have Fun

Candace, my last conference before class, stops and turns as she's leaving and says, "By the way, that new book isn't in the bookstore. They said it might get here next week." My heart rate doubles. In the next three minutes, I have to go to the bathroom, run out to the parking lot to feed the meter, make sure I have all the papers I am supposed to hand out, and come up with something to do in my eighty-minute class, since my carefully planned sequence of writing and discussion periods rested on the assumption that my students would have bought the book and read at least the opening chapter. Years ago, I would have had to struggle against panic at such a moment, but by the time the bathroom door creaks shut behind me, I'm grinning to myself, thinking of the students' upcoming surprise and pleasure, the fun we're going to have.

Don Murray opens the second edition of his classic book *A Writer Teaches Writing* with a "secret": "teaching writing is fun" (1). Because an avalanche of student papers or comparing our salaries to college classmates' may make it difficult to remember the joy inherent in our profession, I have tried throughout this book to remind readers what we get out of our jobs, the basis for Murray's "fun." Most of my ideas involve gradual processes requiring subtle shifts in attitude or slow, painstaking work to enlighten those around us. But sometimes we need a quick fix, an immediate solution to an immediate problem, a way to turn potential disaster into creative engagement with new material. This chapter describes a dozen of my favorite class activities that last from twenty to ninety minutes, require no preparation, and fit usefully into almost any open slot in a writing class.

102

I avoid the word *exercises* in the following to emphasize that we're not just developing writing muscles through meaningless drills; we're discovering and trying out techniques that we can often use later the same day on our own papers. There are no fillers here; these activities produce some of the best classes I can offer students. They engage me and my students, they have significant repercussions for the rest of the semester, and they provide both symbolic and literal evidence that even on a day when all else goes wrong, we invisible faculty members can create memorable and meaningful experiences for our students.

1. Speed through a writing process. This activity strikes me as so universally useful, so fundamental, that I almost didn't include it because I'd like to think that every composition teacher now uses some variation of it. But many senior English majors still tell me they've never spent a class period sampling a sequence of process approaches and have never been exposed to my favorites. So I offer here one of hundreds of ways to experiment with writing processes for sixty minutes.

The general concept is to lead students from blank pages / blank minds to "finished" paragraph in less time than they would have thought possible. I prepare students by saying a little about process theory, emphasizing that we're going to experiment with *a* process, not *the* process. I compare process approaches to a golf bag full of clubs or a mechanic's toolbox—the golfer or mechanic doesn't just settle on a beloved sand wedge or ratchet and use it every time; he or she gets to know all the tools well enough to make an intelligent choice for each particular situation. I tell students that I will be happy if they find one or two approaches that appeal to them and seem to work for them.

Then we're off, usually pursuing some combination of the following.

- **Brainstorm.** List all the subjects that pop into your head at the moment. Don't censor, don't ask if this will work, don't think, What if my parents saw this list? Just get as many down in three or four minutes as you can.

- **Choose.** Which one excites you, surprises you, scares you, confuses you? Which do you NEED to write on?

- **Freewrite on your topic.** Some call this a garbage drill, a vomit-all. James Dickey says for one nugget of gold he has to mine fifty tons of ore, yet most student writers try to get everything perfect the first time and throw nothing away. Don't head for perfection, head for quantity, try to get your pen to keep up with your head, you can't do it but it's fun to try, don't worry about spelling, punctuation, grammar, making sense—follow that tangent, of course this isn't coherent, the point is to break out of the gummy coherent ruts of our normal thinking and come up with something that might be exciting to work on. Phew.

- **Reread the freewrite,** circling or underlining surprises, interesting combinations of words or ideas, phrases you want to keep, tangents that came out of nowhere.

- **Map/web/bubble.** Put a code phrase for your evolving subject — "parents' divorce"—in a circle in the center of a piece of paper, then around it put circles with words that seem immediately related— "blame," "harm to kids," "friends' parents," "our impossible choice," "legal stuff"—then surround each of the second-level bubbles with new bubbles and continue the process until your page is filled with a spiderweb.

- **Analyze your bubbling.** Did a particular bubble—perhaps "our impossible choice" in the example above—get surrounded by a great number of other bubbles, shifting the center of interest away from the original subject? Do any bubbles bumping into each other suggest new connections, new lines of inquiry? Any surprises? Allow yourself to be torn away from the topic you thought you were pursuing. Maybe it would be more fruitful to pursue your relationship with your sister than your parents' divorce.

- **Play with distance.** Close-ups create interest; wide-angle shots provide context, meaning, significance. Start close: create a quick scene, maybe your parents fighting or you and your sister huddled together. Then pull your camera eye back and write a sentence or two of context. Do you want to approach divorce in terms of economics, education, religion, modern society, gender roles, law, family, psychology, anthropology?

- **Title your evolving idea.** How can you title it when you haven't even written it yet? That's the point. Coming up with ten titles in three minutes can show you ten different directions your idea could take, ten different papers. Don't try for the perfect title, the best combination of words—you can work on that later. Try to make your titles as different from one another as possible, to get as many angles as you can on your evolving subject.

- **Choose the best title for the moment,** not the one that will grab a reader or win a pithy title contest, but the one that leads you most clearly in the direction you want to go.

- **Draft.** Using your title, your close-up, and your context, write a paragraph about your subject. Think of it as a summary if you want, or as a lead for a larger paper, or just as the way you would tell a friend about the situation.

- **Revise.** Even when writing in such short segments, you should practice separating the creative from the editorial, spilling out the words and *then* making them right.
- **Share.** In the whole class or in small groups, read aloud what you wrote. This is not the time for criticism. Find something specific that you like.

A series of steps like this makes a good exercise, demonstrating techniques that students can use for the rest of their lives. So it has value even if everyone writes about trivial, irrelevant subjects. But students will put more into it, and it will have more meaning for them, if they're working on an important subject that might turn into a paper or might "count" in some other way. One of the beauties of a multistep approach is that even if you start with an inconsequential subject, something that happens to be stuck in your mind at the moment—the *Simpsons* episode you watched the night before—if you kick it around, associate freely about it, take the project seriously, you're likely to come up with a subject you care about—Homer's resolution to make Bart a man may parallel your own father's bumbling attempts to establish the "right" gender roles for you, and that might be something worth writing about.

2. Tell them a story. (With thanks to Janet Schofield.) No, I'm not suggesting a reversion to grade school, though I'd be glad to import into my writing classes some of the casual intimacy of that period. Many of my students find it difficult to shift from writing high school "exercises," which simply display and practice writing ability, to writing college papers that have a focus, a point, at least a hypothetical reason for being. I spend much of my conference time asking questions intended to get students beyond just telling a story to ponder the meaning or effect they might want that story to have.

For this activity, we exchange roles. We get in a circle, I tell a loose, meandering, pointless story, and the students play teacher, questioning and suggesting, trying as a group to find ways to head the story toward an essay. They find the process satisfying because so often they sit through the long, rambling stories of friends, relatives, and particularly teachers, secretly wanting to get to the pruning and focusing that I encourage in this activity.

I usually describe a big decision I had to make at the end of my junior year in high school. I choose that particular story because it has many possible meanings and students can relate to my indecision, my parents' influence, the details about high school, the shifting allegiances, the mixture of selfishness and idealism. I'm enthusiastically long-winded about some points (I often open with a two-minute description of the red-orange hair and aquamarine mole of one of the main characters) and don't explain other important points at all.

Then I ask for suggestions about what the point or focus might be, and I respond to each one by asking what details would have to be expanded or deleted, what issues made clearer, if I were to turn my story in that particular direction. Students usually overflow with ideas and have no trouble seeing that their particular vision of the essay requires different deletions and additions than did the previous one. The process dispels the notion that any one situation offers just one meaning, one perspective, one focus, one point. And we all benefit from students' having this process under their belts—once they've done it to my story, they can do it to each other's, or I can say in conference, "You need to do to this paper what you guys did to my story in class."

This experiment makes more sense in the first half of the semester, but it fits in any time there are twenty free minutes.

3. Get them smelling. Returning to the sources of writing inspiration almost always pays off—sometimes most handsomely when we're wound up in writing's complexities. Nature writers can imaginatively visit a favorite scene, poets write down dreams, fiction writers list stories they heard as children. And almost everyone can benefit from returning to their senses.

Inspiration can come from anywhere, at any time, but sometimes we can nudge it along by focusing our attention. During a spring fever epidemic or if too many people complain about not being able to come up with anything new, I tell them to go out and smell—spend twenty-five minutes outside (or even inside in an unusual place like a laundry room), silently, by themselves, concentrating on each sense in turn for five minutes, jotting down brief observations to expand on later. This half hour sometimes breaks students of their exclusive use of visual descriptions, and like the next experiment, it can get them to see the world in a grain of sand.

4. Expand a generalization with details. Some students have a difficult time fleshing out their prose. They make a general statement—"freshmen are often lonely"—and then don't see any way to expand it, to *show* as well as *tell.* They sometimes interpret pleas for specifics as requests to pad or bullshit, and in response they often repeat the same idea on the same level of generalization. But when given someone else's generalization and the freedom to draw from experience or to fantasize, many reluctant writers suddenly find that they have more to say.

I put five sentences on the board, "She was a compulsive housecleaner" always among them, since I wrote on that with great pleasure when Margo

She was a compulsive housecleaner; she hated anything that looked, smelled, felt, tasted, or sounded like dirt. But most emphatically, she hated hair. To her, trying to get those clinging, slimy hairs from floor to sponge, from sponge to fingers, and from fingers to toilet bowl, was like trying to throw up when you know you're sick—she knew she'd feel better afterwards, but the act itself was unspeakably repulsive. The life expectancy of a sponge in her house was measured in terms of hours or days rather than weeks or months. After wiping the toothpaste stains off the sink or gritting her teeth and inserting the sponge blindly behind the back of the toilet, she would give the sponge a couple of good rinses and one thorough picking, and if it was still hairy, she often had to leave the room to stifle the urge to throw it into the flushing john. Her toilet was strong, full-bodied, wasteful, perhaps, but effective, and she was fairly sure it could handle a 3 for 89¢ sponge. But the thought of that little pink piece of rotting cellulose stuck in the tubes somewhere, gathering putrid hairs until it looked like a sea anemone in a cesspool, made her shiver with nausea and consign the sponge, with its mates, to the wastebasket.

Figure 11–1. *Staff Meeting Freewrite*

Page introduced me to this experiment (see Figure 11–1). Other sentences I've used include: "It was disgusting to watch him eat," "He was a soap opera addict," and "More than anything, she hated dogs." I tell students they can alter pronouns, and I give them ten minutes to write, starting a paragraph with one of the sentences. Most think of someone they know who fits the generalization, and they endeavor to come up with the most disgusting, most accurate details to describe the eater or the housecleaner.

Students often vie to read their pieces aloud, and classmates respond appreciatively. I try to stress the ability to expand *and* contract by focusing on a particular detail in each piece and pointing out how effective that one detail could be: "If you felt you had space to include only one more sentence about the housecleaner, think of how the single sentence 'She scrubbed the bathroom grout so hard she broke her finger' would add depth to the character." We talk about the blurred line between imagination and experience, and I encourage them to search for the concrete, effective detail for any writing task, inserting real experience into fiction and imagination into nonfiction.

For the rest of the semester, I can prompt students to enliven their vague writing with details by suggesting they do what they did with the compulsive housecleaner.

5. Have students analyze their writing processes. (Inspired by Coe and Gutierrez.) An unfortunate and illogical response to the writing process movement has been the rigidification of a particular writing process by some teachers and textbooks. I don't think any of the movement's pioneers would say that there is a right process, wrong process, or best process; the right process is what works for an individual writer facing a specific writing task, allowing that writer to produce, without too much sweat and trauma, work that pleases the writer and the audience. The same process might not work for the same writer on the next assignment and might never be useful for the writer at the next desk.

The alternative to prescribing the "best" process is to examine the current process(es) of individual writers, try to figure out what steps work and what steps are painful or counterproductive, and expand, change, or eliminate steps based on their track record. Students can perform such an analysis largely on their own, though at some point the teacher can help by examining the results and making suggestions about what's unusual, what seems to be working, and what alternatives might ease students through their difficulties.

Students need only a blank piece of paper and some memory of the process they went through writing a particular piece some time in the recent past. I list here the questions I've most recently asked students to consider on a beginning-of-the-semester analysis, but depending on time constraints, the list could be significantly expanded or reduced.

1. Why did I write this paper?
2. How did I come up with the subject?
3. Who did I talk to about my subject?
4. How did I refine the subject?
5. What did I do to plan the paper before the first draft?
6. What tools (e.g., red pen, yellow pad, computer) did I use?
7. How did I make the first draft into a final draft?
8. How did I come up with my opening paragraph?
9. Who read the drafts?
10. What reaction did I get from my teacher or other reader?
11. What parts of the process were difficult or painful?
12. What parts were easy or enjoyable?
13. What is usually the hardest step in the writing process for me? Be ready to discuss in conference ways to experiment with that step to find alternatives.
14. What is my personal writing goal for the semester?

I like to leave students time to go back over their answers and judge whether each step is part of their "normal" process, marking *T* for typical and *U* for unusual. They then go through a final time and determine which steps they'd most like to change.

It's important for students to answer some of the opening questions in order to remember as clearly as possible what they wrote, why, and how, but for me the crucial questions are the last few. I try to get students to take as much responsibility for their writing improvement as possible, defining for themselves their own goals (which might range from "procrastinate less" to "learn to be more concise"), pinpointing what really gives them trouble and, before they come to me for a prescription, thinking about how else they might handle the troublesome steps.

This analysis takes a minimum of fifteen minutes, though it could productively be expanded to two hours or more. I like to devote twenty or thirty minutes just to an exchange of "hardest steps." Often one student has conquered the problem that stymies another and can suggest solutions that might be better than mine or more readily accepted.

I usually have students analyze their processes a second time near the end of the course, commenting on changes, insights, resolutions for the future.

6. Play with voice. Whether students are struggling to break out of the dull-and-distant research paper voice they developed in high school or to find a way to make their essay more personal and engaging, they can benefit from exploring voice for a class period. In one of my favorite voice experiments, everyone writes about a subject we all have in common—high school. First, we see ourselves as failures and dredge up details for "Portrait of the Artist as a Young Loser." Then we take the same experience, if possible the same details, and write a success story, a *Bildungsroman* of the young hero. After this warm-up, we write two or three other quick notes or letters—to a loved or hated teacher, an old friend or an old enemy, the principal or the classmate we never had the nerve to speak to.

This may be the most therapeutic writing activity I know. In ten minutes, we accomplish what much modern therapy attempts to do in years—we tell positive stories about events that we've seen negatively in the past. Doing it for five minutes obviously isn't a substitute for years on the psychiatrist's couch, but it is intriguing to see how easy it is to switch perspectives, sometimes while staring straight at the same subject—"my boyfriend situation in high school" or "my adolescence on sports fields." Once you do it, you wonder whether lack of will or creativity keeps us from performing such mental reversals in "real life"—or whether it just never occurs to us to try.

If students feel more comfortable taking on a role, constructing a voice from which they can distance themselves, we can ask them to put on masks, adopt voices. Ballenger sets up a funny situation—a gentleman gets out of a taxi and steps in dog poop—and has students tell the story first in the gentleman's words, then in the taxi driver's (1993, 144). Students writing about political subjects can have fun taking on a radical and identifiable voice for a page—Rush Limbaugh or Chairman Mao. Whatever the specifics we use, we need to emphasize *play* and try to ensure that students have a real interest in either the subject or the voice.

7. Read with the class . . . very slowly. Writers need to understand what readers do, and to explore the reading process we need to slow it down so we can see the hundreds of things our brains do as they process every word. For this experiment I need about forty minutes and a copy of a favorite narrative poem, either on paper or in my head. Paul Slayton demonstrated this technique using Gwendolyn Brooks' poem "Sadie and Maud"; I usually do it with Langston Hughes' "Ballad of the Girl Whose Name Is Mud."

Ballad of the Girl Whose Name Is Mud

A girl with all that raising,
It's hard to understand
How she could get in trouble
With a no-good man.

The guy she gave her all to
Dropped her with a thud.
Now amongst decent people,
Dorothy's name is mud.

But nobody's seen her shed a tear,
Nor seen her hang her head.
Ain't even heard her murmur,
Lord, I wish I was dead!

No! The hussy's telling everybody—
Just as though it was no sin—
That if she had a chance
She'd do it agin'!

I introduce ultraslow reading by raising one of the crucial questions for all education: How do we get ideas and information from our very limited short-term memory to long-term memory, storing it in a way we can retrieve it? My one-sentence answer: Connect the new to the known. We see how we make such connections as we read the poem.

I write the title of the poem on the board and ask for associations, feelings for the tone of the poem, guesses about what's going to happen. Everyone has connections with *ballad,* ideas about what "the girl" might have done to be named *mud,* a sense from the title that the poem will mix serious and funny.

As I solicit reactions to individual words and we unfold the story one line at a time, we find that seemingly idiosyncratic reactions ("My mother used *raising* that way, and she was from Alabama") often lead to useful inferences. We realize that because of our different associations, we all in effect read different poems, and the more conscious we are of where our associations and connotations come from, the better readers we can be. We learn that small, simple words (like *all* in the line "the guy she gave her all to") can pack a lot of meaning and may be more effective than ten-dollar words.

In the remainder of the class period (or, if necessary, at the next class meeting), I ask students to suggest what the process teaches us about reading and writing, and eventually I give them the handout shown in Figure 11–2.

8. Lead students through a descriptive outline. Students need a paper to work on for this experiment, the best method I've found for helping writers see and change the structure of their papers. It can be used at all but the first

---

What can we learn about reading?

1. As we read, we develop predictions and expectations that are subsequently fulfilled or frustrated.

2. Our expectations depend on our personal associations with the words of the text. Some associations might be unique to us, while some we share with other members of our age group, nationality, family, religion, race, bowling team . . . .

3. Our brain makes many associations and connections automatically, but we can read better and remember better if we make connections consciously, actively.

4. The associations provoked in us by a text are never "stupid" or "wrong"; they make sense. One set of associations is about as logical as another. (Whether our associations resemble the author's is a different question.)

5. We should trust our reading instincts.

6. Because of the uniqueness of our different associations, each of us in essence reads a different text.

Figure 11–2. *"Ballad" Follow-Up*

(*continued on next page*)

7. We read more quickly and remember more if we are well prepared before we read with a knowledge of the text's purpose and context.

8. We need to make distinctions between the views expressed by the characters or implied by the narrator, and the views of the characters' creator.

What can we learn about writing?

1. Setting up the right expectations is crucial: form, genre, title, lead, headings, signposts, even neatness.

2. Start with a known and agreed-upon aspect of the issue.

3. Give the reader the big picture.

4. Accept that your words will reveal more than you're aware of.

5. You can't control a word's connotations, much less individuals' associations with the word, so stick with words whose connotations you know and want.

6. The best word is often short and simple.

Examples of connecting the new to the known

1. Mnemonic devices; most memorization techniques.

2. Speed reading.

3. Studying-for-exam techniques.

4. Learning foreign languages.

5. Describing something new: "it's like . . . ."

6. Cross-disciplinary education: connecting English, history, art history, sociology, psychology, religion. . . .

7. Most of the reading and writing lessons above.

8. Poetry.

Figure 11–2. (*continued*)

stages of writing, and on any kind of paper. The goal is to resee the paper, its parts, and its connections and to focus revision on issues of content and organization. Even when I give the class a step-by-step handout like the one in Figure 11–3, I talk them through each step, on the board creating an outline of a paper of mine that they've read.

1. **Number each paragraph.** This is the only thing you do on the paper itself. This activity shifts attention away from the individual pages of the paper and focuses it on the paper's skeleton. It's much easier to get a sense of the whole when we can see the entire paper on one page.

2. **On a clean sheet of paper, jot down a number for each paragraph, spacing evenly** (i.e., if you have twenty paragraphs, number them one through twenty).

3. **Summarize each paragraph in as few words as possible.** Write each summary next to the appropriate number.

4. **Reflect on what you just did.** Why were certain paragraphs difficult to summarize? Are they unfocused or incoherent or compound? Should you break a paragraph into two? Did you find you could use ditto marks because a number of paragraphs in a row were about the same subject? Does the subject deserve that much attention? Could someone glancing at the summaries of your opening and closing paragraphs get a sense of how they connect?

5. **Group the summaries into blocks.** Use brackets or different colors or whatever works. First get every summary into a group, then bracket some of those groups into larger blocks until you get to the one block that they all fit under. Label each group.

6. **Reflect again.** Are some summaries out of place, requiring you to draw an arrow to the correct group? Does the number of paragraphs in each block roughly correspond to the relative importance of that block? You have now created a kind of an outline sometimes called a tree diagram. Do its major blocks correspond to what you see as the major sections in your paper? Are you missing parts? Do the blocks appear in the best order?

7. **Mark junctions between blocks and summarize what the transition at each spot needs to do.** Between every pair of blocks, big and small, there should be some indication of a change of subjects: a paragraph break or a bullet if not some kind of verbal transition. Resist the temptation to see what transition you *did* use. First figure out what *should* be there, then see if you can find it in the paper.

8. **Write down all the changes you want to make.** This process in effect X-rays the draft, and this new form of seeing can open your eyes to many kinds of re-vision, not just organizational rearrangement.

Figure 11–3. *Descriptive Outline*

This activity works even better if the class has a chance to try out the approach on a piece of professional writing. I sometimes have the class read Caroline Bird's "Where College Fails Us" and then I assign pairs of students two paragraphs to summarize on the board. The resulting outline not only shows students the simple structure of a seemingly complex article, it helps them see the gaps and logic problems in a professional piece and prepares them to argue with it.

9. Analyze leads. We know how important the lead or opener of any piece of writing is. It establishes the tone, voice, and direction of the piece. It's the part most casual readers sample before deciding to read the whole piece or to move on. Leads often give a strong and accurate sense of the whole article. When I have classes choose their favorite leads from an anonymous list of their classmates', they often pick the leads from the papers that got the best grades.

But what part of the lead grabs us, convinces us to read on? Many writers give suggestions about what could or should be in a lead (see, for instance, Munter [56] and any of Murray's books), but it's more satisfying for an individual or the whole class to figure out, based on their own taste and judgment, what works in leads they read.

For this experiment, everyone needs a copy of the same reading anthology or packet. The teacher chooses eight or ten pieces that the class hasn't read and tells everyone to read the first paragraph (or the first page, or the first inch) fairly quickly, jot down an impression or two, and move on to the next. Everyone votes for a favorite lead, and then the whole class spends ten to forty minutes discussing why they chose a particular lead, what interested them in other leads or turned them off. We try to end up with a board full of generalizations about what works in a lead.

An energetic teacher can collect a lead from each student, copy them all in one handout, and go through a similar process with student leads. Often just reading their lead in the context of others opens writers' eyes and provokes them to resolve to make changes.

10. Exchange papers randomly. Of the scores of ways to get peer feedback to student writers, this one has long been my favorite, and it's equally popular with students. Students need to have a draft to exchange, one of the reasons I encourage them, after the first month or so, to bring to class every day a draft to work on. The activity takes a whole class period—up to ninety minutes.

I put on the board or hand out a list of questions or prompts for readers to respond to, and I ask each author to write a question of his or her own on the first or last page. My lists vary somewhat depending on the class, but they usually include

1. The author's name
2. The reader's perception of the point or theme or focus of the paper (the answer to the "So What?" question)
3. The strengths of the paper (specific and general)
4. Things that confused the reader
5. The authors' question (often "Does it flow?" or "Does the end make sense?").

Students sit in a circle and, to begin, pass their papers to the second person on their left. Everyone reads that first paper and responds anonymously to the questions on a blank piece of paper, a fresh page (or half-page) for each paper. After a particular student has read and responded to one paper, he or she either puts the paper in a central "hat" and retrieves another or looks around the room until someone else is finished, at which point the two exchange. The process continues until seven or eight minutes before the end of the class period, when I ask everyone to bring the responses up to my desk. Then I play mailman, sorting the responses into piles for each author.

Students like to read a number of their classmates' papers, to see what others are working on, and they usually enjoy receiving a variety of feedback as well. They consider the anonymous comments more honest than the face-to-face reactions they get in revision groups, and they often take suggestions to heart. I caution, "You're the author, you have to make the final decisions yourself," but I add that if a section confuses more than one reader, that section should change. The process could be abused by vicious students eager to attack classmates, but I've never had that happen.

11. Let them gripe. When asked "What do you like to write?" many students list only "letters." I encourage letter writing because I would love to spread to other genres the relaxed, playful, willing-to-experiment attitude that most people bring to that three-page note they dashed off to their old roommate while procrastinating about a lab report.

I also share with most of my students a fondness for griping and a feeling of being powerless to do anything about abuse from anonymous people and faceless corporations. So this activity provides a small sense of power as well as good practice in writing with a specific purpose and audience in mind; it may encourage students to speak up for their rights in other areas of life.

I prime the class by reading and/or discussing some of my own gripes. I usually start with the situation that made me a fan of the gripe letter, an exchange of a dozen letters with Toyota in the mid 1970s that convinced the auto giant to pay for a valve job caused by its admitted, though unpublicized, design error. That $120 check was motivation to write the cereal company when I found sticks in my breakfast bowl, the breadmaker when I found "foreign matter" in my loaf, the insulation company that didn't put enough nails in the weatherstripping bag, the truck rental company whose truck leaked, the tape deck manufacturer when the local shop couldn't fix the deck—all with results that made the effort worthwhile. I expand the concept of "gripe" by discussing a few letters to the editor and to bosses and administrators. Then I ask for student stories. Often a surprising number have had similar small successes. I warn against two industries that don't seem to mind leaving their customers angry—computers and airlines—and then I give students time to write their own.

Writing these letters provides a good break any time in the semester; if I do it early, I try to get as many students as possible to send the letters off so that they can share the results with the rest of us. In any case, many students enjoy blowing off steam and putting on paper the rant that's been in their heads, and they feel a sense of triumph just reading their invective aloud. Of course they need to be cautioned to reread their letters, have someone else read them, and sleep on them before they actually send them off. But I have yet to run into a problem with a student sending a too-aggressive letter, and the activity provides excellent opportunities to talk about purpose, tone, and audience, when to be angry, when to assume agreement, when to let facts speak for themselves.

12. Learn from other processes. For some students, writing is an alien process. Maybe once it felt natural, but it became uncomfortable and foreign as people started criticizing and GRAMMAR became a big issue, and they used writing only in times of stress. Often such students have learned to do just what the teacher wants, like trained monkeys, and without instruction they're lost.

It's worth spending time to help such students relax with a process that is, after all, almost as natural as speaking. Have them think about processes that they're intimate and comfortable with—kicking a football, sketching a nude, learning a dance step, barbecuing ribs, teaching a swimming stroke, rigging a sailboat. They need some time to jot down a number of such processes and choose one; then they list the steps involved in that process and try to draw connections between those steps and the process of writing. They may notice, for instance, that watching videotapes of the previous game's field goal attempts is like rereading the last draft to discover its strengths and weaknesses; that they don't put off thinking about a process they enjoy, but cook it over in their minds long before it's apparently necessary; that some of the advice they give to kids in their swimming classes they need to take themselves when writing.

I don't go around the room talking about processes in a single class period, because after four or five people have spoken, others are likely to pick up on their precedents and say similar things. I prefer to have everyone jot down their own thoughts for a few minutes, learning from their own processes, and then have half a dozen volunteers talk. I encourage each successive one to mention a different kind of relationship between the two processes, a different kind of learning.

I regularly borrow classroom activities from others, and I trust that readers will borrow ideas from this book. But I think most of us need classroom suggestions less than we need the confidence that we can come up with surprising pedagogical successes simply by responding creatively to the moment. As I was in the last revisions of this book, just before Halloween, Sylvia Edwards, a Humanities professor from Longview Community College in Kansas City, posted on the ECOMP-L listserve a plea for "treats" from other instructors; she felt she was out of "tricks." I wrote back that she should "figure out what you could do tomorrow in class that would be the most fun FOR YOU." She responded: "Purely by accident this fun happened today." Her students had written a grueling gen. ed. assessment essay, then

> My challenge was figuring out how to use the left over 35 minutes. I supplied them with scissors, magazines, post-it notes, paper clips, etc and told each established group to examine magazine ads and to create a picture essay on the image of men and women the ads created. I spent Sunday creating my own models.
>
> As a bonus one of the students sweetened the pot by bringing donuts for everyone. I don't know if it was a sugar or creative high, but spirits were definitely higher as the class ended.

I hope the same is true for readers of this book.

Epilogue
A Three-Class Day

Freewriting in my 9:00 A.M. class, I start board-musing about whether I should have been an accountant—flouting the stereotype of people in creative fields, I enjoy balancing my checkbook, making lists and checking things off, even doing my taxes. Unless I'm struggling to understand the tortured logic of an IRS form, it's soothing, low-energy work. On the other hand, I don't think I could feel good about my life if I chewed numbers all day; checking "checkbook" off the list doesn't fulfill the same needs as writing a page.

As I write titles about the same subject, I go from "Poet versus Accountant" to "Creative versus Mechanical," and by the time I get to "Right Brain and Left Brain" I've developed new insights into the reasons that different kinds of work give me different kinds of pleasure. And I've recognized the profound and obvious fact that I should think of my pleasures not in *versus* but in *and* terms.

In my 10:30 class, I list "telemarking" as something I know about, and "The Intimacy of the Chairlift" appears in my title list. I freewrite about my ride on the world's slowest chairlift at Gunstock with a guy who had an artificial voice box. I feel foolish never to have thought about ski tow as social setting, though I've spent thirty-six winters riding T-bars and chairs and Pomas and gondolas and trams and rope tows and skimobiles. The insights about chair lifts don't change my life, but I think I'll get a poem out of them.

At lunchtime, an English education student from last semester stops in to chat and tells me how he'd never gotten anything out of a writing course until he'd seen me up at the board not talking about writing but writing, thinking, discovering and developing ideas, remembering things long forgotten, making new connections. Writing and watching me write, he had discovered both why he wanted to write and how he wanted to teach.

In the afternoon, I lead my Teaching Writing class through the Descriptive Outline (number 8 in Chapter 11). They work hard, but they don't say much until Natalie, one of the sharpest and most talkative people in class, looks up with a frown and says, "Does this work better with some things than others? I'm having a really hard time with it."

Years ago, Natalie's question would have rung in my head as I walked to my car; her doubt would have dominated my psyche. It still bothers me enough to make me try to think of a better answer. But I'm not deflated.

I can retain my equilibrium better now not just because I'm more experienced or doing better work or becoming callused to criticism. Some favorite activities like the Descriptive Outline I've been doing in consistent ways for years, and if the quality of presentation has changed, it has gotten worse because of a slow ebbing of genuine discovery and freshness.

I can cling to a more positive attitude now largely because I know what some of the silent students are thinking:

"I really didn't know what my paper said until we did that."

"I think I've got it organized now."

"That's the most helpful thing I've learned in a writing class."

"I tried it out on my management paper and realized I needed to use headings."

"It's so much easier to see everything on a single page."

I've heard enough fragmentary, throwing-the-bookbag-over-the-shoulder testimonials to know now that despite Natalie's challenge and the puzzled, blank, disengaged faces of her classmates, at least half of them will leave class thinking of organization, revision, writing itself in a new way, and many of their papers will grow in response.

Brandee will scrap the paper about her sister's wedding and dig into the significance of her grandfather's attendance, turning an extended description into a wrenching portrait of a working man whose mind will no longer let him work and of a granddaughter learning from his example both the value of work and the dangers of an addiction to it.

Having discovered her real subject in a long ramble about the joys of playing in the fields when she was a kid, Tina will confront directly her love-hate relationship with busyness and responsibility and develop some long-overdue self-tolerance.

I haven't read those revisions by the time I leave the class; no one says a word about insights and breakthroughs. But I know they're there, just as I'm confident similar silent changes have occurred today in the minds and writings of composition instructors' students around the country.

I'm not Mr. Upbeat, smiling and clicking my heels as I walk down the linoleum away from the class. I'm thinking about Natalie's comment, planning my opening remarks for the next class, trying to imagine how I'm going to get through all the papers I'm supposed to read by Monday. But with scores of classes under my belt and this book in my back pocket, I do indulge myself in the most delicious, forbidden satisfaction for the composition instructor: I allow myself to think, "That was a great class."

Annotated Bibliography

Ballenger, Bruce. 1998. *The Curious Researcher.* 2nd revised ed. Boston: Allyn & Bacon.

This welcome alternative to standard research texts prompts students to explore their own curiosity and create a researched essay. Good writing, an engaging voice, a process orientation, and lively examples make this the book that keeps instructors from dreading the research segment of first-year English courses.

Ballenger, Bruce, and Barry Lane. 1989. *Discovering the Writer Within.* Cincinnati: Writer's Digest.

Subtitled "40 days to more imaginative writing," this collaboration provides creative, quirky, inspiring ideas that anyone can use and that help thousands of instructors perk up their classes.

Christensen, Francis, and Bonniejean Christensen. 1978. *Notes Toward a New Rhetoric: Nine Essays for Teachers.* New York: Harper.

This slim volume includes fascinating studies that should, among other things, put to rest forever the prohibition on and *and* but *as sentence openers.*

Dethier, Brock. 1983. "In Defense of Subjective Grading." *North Carolina English Teacher* 40 (4): 3-6.

Someone had to say it: subjectivity is a writing teacher's strength, not something to be embarrassed about.

Elbow, Peter. 1993. "Ranking, Evaluating, and Liking: Sorting Out Three Forms of Judgment." *College English* 55: 187-206.

Provocative article about our relationships with our students and how we evaluate them. Elbow's work is always worth reading.

————. 1973. *Writing Without Teachers.* New York: Oxford.

This tremendously influential book introduced the world to freewriting, teacherless classes, and "the doubting game and the believing game."

Fitzgerald, Kathryn, Heather Bruce, Sharon Stasney, and Anna Vogt. 1998. *Conversations in Context: Identity, Knowledge, and College Writing.* Fort Worth: Harcourt.

One of a new generation of readers that build on the insights of social construc-tionism, this book acknowledges and tries to overcome the sense of alienation that most students feel when trying to write in the strange worlds of academic dis-course. It challenges students to think in fresh ways about their identities and their place in academic life, and it helps them join academic discussions by ex-amining the making of meaning and the types of writing in different disciplines.

Fletcher, Ralph. 1993. *What a Writer Needs.* Portsmouth, NH: Boynton/Cook.

Fletcher writes so well, with a great memory for relevant anecdotes and quota-tions, that he brings new life to discussions of some of the prerequisites for good writing—mentors, a love of words, the art of specificity.

Flower, Linda. 1993. *Problem-Solving Strategies for Writing.* 4th ed. New York: Harcourt.

Flower has been a major force in composition research over the past twenty years, and I find her distinction between "writer-based" and "reader-based" prose tremendously useful. Student writers need to progress from a solipsistic "writer-based" focus ("I had a really hard time finding any information about my topic . . . ") to think about what their readers need to hear.

Gaughan, John. 1997. *Cultural Reflections: Critical Teaching and Learning in the English Classroom.* Portsmouth: Boynton/Cook.

One of two books (the other being Pirie's, below) that have helped me see how a process perspective can be integrated with social constructionist insights in the English class. Gaughan shows how to mix media, genres, reading, and writing in English courses that help students not only write better but understand them-selves and their place in the world better.

Lopate, Phillip. 1994. *The Art of the Personal Essay.* New York: Doubleday.

Though too massive (777 pages) to use for most writing classes, this collection rep-resents a big step in the revival of the essay as a popular genre. Its historical orga-nization and multicultural breadth make it very useful for writing teachers who like to know more about the genre they teach than the typical freshman reader can tell them.

Macrorie, Ken. 1996. *Uptaught.* Portsmouth: Boynton/Cook.

Macrorie helped the composition world loosen up in the early '70s, when this book first appeared, and his voice hasn't lost its appeal. His concept Engfish *should be in every vocabulary.*

Munter, Mary. 1996. *Guide to Managerial Communication.* 4th ed. Englewood Cliffs, NJ: Prentice-Hall.

An excellent book that provides a business slant to teaching writing and speaking.

Murray, Donald. 1998. *Write to Learn*. 6th ed. Fort Worth: Harcourt.
The *First-year Writing text.*

————. 1997. *The Craft of Revision*. 3d ed. Fort Worth: Harcourt.
Resistance to revision cripples many student writers, and this streamlined text provides the best cure I know. Includes particularly lively and useful interviews with a variety of writers.

————. 1993. *Read to Learn*. 3d ed. Fort Worth: Harcourt.
Murray weaves enough process ideas and activities into this reader to make it a good choice as the only text in a writing course. He shows us superb writing in process, something students don't see often enough.

————. 1990. *Shoptalk: Learning to Write with Writers*. Portsmouth, NH: Boynton/Cook.
Great collection of quotations from writers. Borrow one a day to write on the board, and students will think you know your stuff.

————. 1989. *Expecting the Unexpected: Teaching Myself—and Others—to Read and Write*. Portsmouth, NH: Boynton/Cook.
An excellent collection of classic Murray pieces.

————. 1985. *A Writer Teaches Writing*. Boston: Houghton Mifflin.
My Teaching Writing students see this book as a godsend. Chapters 2 and 3 contain a complete writing course, Murray handles with typical honesty and directness many of the difficult issues that writing teachers face, and even the short section on computers doesn't seem particularly dated. The best single book in the composition teacher's library.

————. 1982. *Learning by Teaching*. Montclair, NJ: Boynton/Cook.
"Selected articles on writing and teaching."

Nelson, Marie. 1991. *At the Point of Need*. Portsmouth, NH: Boynton/Cook.
Nelson describes the evolution of her group workshop approach for basic and ESL writers, along the way reaching a number of interesting conclusions about working with writers at every level. Intelligent, thoughtful, sensitive treatment of difficult issues.

Newkirk, Thomas, ed. 1993. *Nuts and Bolts: A Practical Guide to Teaching College Composition*. Portsmouth, NH: Boynton/Cook.
Eight of my former UNH colleagues contributed to this collection of engaging, well-tested, student-centered ideas about every aspect of teaching composition from getting started to teaching the research paper to evaluating.

Noguchi, Rei R. 1991. *Grammar and the Teaching of Writing*. Urbana, IL: NCTE.

In light of the failures of traditional grammar instruction, Noguchi suggests alternative ways of teaching sentence boundaries, offering fresh suggestions about handling comma splices and fragments.

Pirie, Bruce. 1997. *Reshaping High School English.* Urbana, IL: NCTE.
Though only partly focused on writing, this book is reshaping my thinking about everything from how to use recent reading theory to the value of the hierarchical expository essay.

Power, Brenda Miller, and Ruth Shagoury Hubbard. 1996. *Oops: What We Learn When Our Teaching Fails.* York, ME: Stenhouse.
This quirky, wonderful book full of interesting in-the-trenches stories encourages us to learn from our failures as well as our successes.

Rief, Linda. 1992. *Seeking Diversity: Language Arts with Adolescents.* Portsmouth, NH: Boynton/Cook.
Rief, who teaches eighth grade, is an idol for many teachers in New England. Must reading for junior high teachers.

Romano, Tom. 1995. *Writing with Passion.* Portsmouth, NH: Boynton/Cook.

———. 1987. *Clearing the Way: Working with Teenage Writers.* Portsmouth, NH: Boynton/Cook.
Both of Romano's books argue passionately (of course) for the value of "rendering" experience with poetry or fiction, for the multigenre research paper, for being human and humane with students. Romano's writing voice captures his personal energy, and his sometimes radical ideas challenge readers to rethink their own approaches.

Shaughnessy, Mina. 1977. *Errors and Expectations.* New York: Oxford.
A must for anyone dealing with "basic writers."

Tate, Gary, Edward P. J. Corbett, and Nancy Myers. 1994. *The Writing Teacher's Sourcebook.* 3d ed. New York: Oxford University Press.
This edition includes several good pieces in sections such as "perspectives," "teachers," "classrooms," "assigning and responding."

Tobin, Lad. 1993. *Writing Relationships: What Really Happens in the Composition Class.* Portsmouth, NH: Boynton/Cook.
Wonderfully honest, thoughtful, groundbreaking book about the relational webs in which the writing teacher works and how those webs affect everything from grading to small-group functioning.

Tobin, Lad, and Thomas Newkirk. 1994. *Taking Stock: The Writing Process Movement in the '90s*. Portsmouth, NH: Boynton/Cook.
You thought the process approach had run its course? Think again.

Weaver, Constance. 1996. *Teaching Grammar in Context*. Portsmouth: Boynton/Cook.
Weaver meticulously demolishes traditional justifications for teaching grammar out of context and provides teachers with both a theoretical framework and some practical minilessons for teaching grammar in the writing class. I arm all my English ed. students with this book before I send them out to deal with school boards and parents.

Wells, Judy. 1991. *The Part-Time Teacher*. Willits, CA: Rainy Day Women Press. (Available through Judy Wells, 2317 B Carleton St., Berkeley, CA 94704).
The titles alone make me smile with anticipation: "The part-time teacher sneaks xerox copies"; "The part-time teacher discusses her students while her mate sleeps"; "The part-time teacher needs a benefactor."

Williams, Joseph. 1997. *Style—Ten Lessons in Clarity and Grace*. 5th ed. New York: Longman.
Lives up to its title—fascinating dissection of sentences and how they work. The best book on style I know.

Works Cited

AAUP KSU Full-Time Non-Tenure Faculty Bargaining Unit. 1998. Available <wysiwyg://13/http://www.trumbull.kent.edu/~aaup/nontenur.html>. 8 July 1998.

AAUP KSU Full-Time Non-Tenure Faculty Bargaining Unit. 1996. Collective Bargaining Agreement. Available <http://www.trumbull.kent.edu/~aaup/nttcba.html>. 8 July 1998.

American Association of University Professors. Guidelines for Good Practice Part-Time and Non-Tenure-Track Faculty. Available <http:// www.igc.apc.org/aaup/ptguide.htm>. 8 July 1998.

American Association of University Professors. Part-Time and Non-Tenure-Track Faculty. Available <http://www.igc.apc.org/aaup/ptlink.htm>. 8 July 1998.

American Association of University Professors. 1997. Statement from the Conference on the Growing Use of Part-Time and Adjunct Faculty. Available <http://www.igc.apc.org/aaup/ptconf.htm>. 8 July 1998.

American Association of University Professors. 1993. The Status of Non-Tenure-Track Faculty. Available <http://www.igc.apc.org/aaup/rbnonten.htm>. 8 July 1998.

AFT Higher Education Department. "Can We Help the Full-Time Professoriate Grow Again, While, At the Same Time, Organizing and Representing Part-Time and Other Nontenure-Track Faculty?" (Part 1), The Vanishing Professor. Available <http://www.aft.org/higheduc/professor/part4.htm>. 17 November 1998.

AFT Higher Education Department. "Can We Help the Full-Time Professoriate Grow Again, While, At the Same Time, Organizing and Representing Part-Time and Other Nontenure-Track Faculty?" (Part 2), The Vanishing Professor. Available <http://www.aft.org/higheduc/professor/part4a.htm>. 17 November 1998.

AFT Higher Education Department. "Statement on Part-Time Faculty Employment." Available <http://www.aft.org/higheduc/parttime. htm>. 17 November 1998.

Applebome, Peter. 1996. "N.C.A.A. Effort to Raise Academic Standards Leaves Many Top Students on Sidelines." New York Times, 23 October, B12.

Atwell, Nancie. 1987. *In the Middle: Writing, Reading, and Learning with Adolescents.* Portsmouth: Boynton/Cook.

Ballenger, Bruce. 1993. "Teaching the Research Paper." In *Nuts and Bolts,* edited by Thomas Newkirk, 129–50. Portsmouth, NH: Boynton/Cook.

Ballenger, Bruce, and Barry Lane. 1989. *Discovering the Writer Within.* Cincinnati: Writer's Digest.

Belenky, Mary Field, Blythe McVicker Clinchy, Nancy Rule Goldberger, and Jill Mattuck Tarule. 1986. *Women's Ways of Knowing.* New York: Basic.

Bird, Caroline. 1997. "Where College Fails Us." In *A Writer's Reader,* edited by Donald Hall and D. L. Emblen, 62–70. 8th ed. New York: Longman.

Bishop, Wendy. 1990. *Something Old, Something New.* Carbondale: Southern Illinois University Press.

Bloom, Lynn Z. 1997. "Why I (Used to) Hate to Give Grades." *College Composition and Communication* 48: 360–71.

Boyer, Ernest L. 1990. *Scholarship Reconsidered: Priorities of the Professoriate.* Princeton, NJ: Carnegie.

Brooke, Robert. 1987. "Underlife and Writing Instruction." *College Composition and Communication* 38: 141–53.

Carroll, James. 1996. "An American Requiem." *Atlantic Monthly* (April): 76–84.

Clabaugh, Gary K., and Edward G. Rozycki. 1996. "Foundations of Education and the Devaluation of Teacher Preparation." In *The Teacher Educator's Handbook,* edited by Frank B. Murray, 395–418. San Francisco: Jossey-Bass.

Coe, Richard M., and Kris Gutierrez. 1981. "Using Problem-Solving Procedures and Process Analysis to Help Students with Writing Problems." *College Composition and Communication* 32: 262–71.

Conference on College Composition and Communication. 1989. *Statement of Principles and Standards for the Postsecondary Teaching of Writing.* Urbana, IL: NCTE.

Constitution of the Non-Tenure-Track Division of the American Association of University Professors Kent State Chapter: 6 pp. Available <http://www.trumbull.kent.edu/~aaup/ nttconst.html>. 8 July 1998.

Coupland, Douglas. 1991. *Generation X.* New York: St. Martin's Press.

Darling-Hammond, Linda, and Velma L. Cobb. 1996. "The Changing Context of Teacher Education." In *The Teacher Educator's Handbook,* edited by Frank B. Murray, 14–62. San Francisco: Jossey-Bass.

Dethier, Brock. 1997. "To Know the Music Is to Reach the Child." *Christian Science Monitor,* 1 July, 18.

————. 1991. "Using Music as a Second Language." *English Journal* 8 (8): 72–76.

————. 1988. *Resources for Writing with a Purpose.* Boston: Houghton Mifflin.

————. 1983. "In Defense of Subjective Grading." *North Carolina English Teacher* 40 (4): 3–6.

Diller, Ann, Barbara Houston, Kathryn Pauly Morgan, Maryann Ayim. 1996. *The Gender Question in Education.* Boulder: Westview.

Donmoyer, Robert. 1996. "The Concept of a Knowledge Base." In *The Teacher Educator's Handbook,* edited by Frank B. Murray, 92–119. San Francisco: Jossey-Bass.

Eccles, Jacquelynne, and Allan Wigfield. 1985. "Teacher Expectations and Student Motivation." In *Teacher Expectancies,* edited by Jerome B. Dusek, 185–226. Hillsdale, NJ: Erlbaum.

Edwards, Sylvia. 1998. E-mail to the author, 3 November.

Ehrenfeld, David. 1994. "Forgetting." In *Paper Graders,* edited by Barry Roberts Greer, 7–15. Corvallis, OR: Cairn Press.

Elbow, Peter. 1993. "Ranking, Evaluating, and Liking: Sorting Out Three Forms of Judgment." *College English* 55: 187–206.

————. 1983. "Embracing Contraries in the Teaching Process." *College English* 45: 327–39.

————. 1973. Writing Without Teachers. New York: Oxford.

Emig, Janet. 1983. *The Web of Meaning: Essays on Writing, Teaching, Learning, and Thinking.* Upper Montclair, NJ: Boynton/Cook.

Fitzgerald, F. Scott. 1945. "The Crack-Up." In *The Crack-Up,* 69–84. New York: New Directions.

Fletcher, Ralph. 1993. *What a Writer Needs.* Portsmouth, NH: Boynton/Cook.

Freire, Paulo. 1970. *Pedagogy of the Oppressed.* New York: Herder.

Gappa, Judith M., and David W. Leslie. 1993. *The Invisible Faculty.* San Francisco: Jossey-Bass.

Glassick, Charles E., Mary Taylor Huber, and Gene I. Maeroff. 1997. *Scholarship Assessed: Evaluation of the Professoriate.* San Francisco: Jossey-Bass.

Godwin, Gail. 1977. "Watcher at the Gate." *New York Times,* 9 January, VII 31.

Greer, Barry R., ed. 1994. *Paper Graders: Notes from the Academic Underclass.* Corvallis, OR: Cairn Press. (Available through <greerb@lbcc.cc.or.us>.)

Hairston, Maxine. 1986. "On Not Being a Composition Slave." In *Training the New Teacher of College Composition,* edited by Charles W. Bridges, 117–24. Urbana, IL: NCTE.

Hickman, John N. 1998. "Adjunct U." *New Republic* (December 7): 14–16.

Jordan, June. 1985. "Nobody Mean More to Me Than You and the Future Life of Willie Jordan." In *On Call,* 123–39. Boston: South End Press.

Kelly, Walt. 1959. *Ten Ever-Lovin' Blue-Eyed Years with Pogo.* New York: Simon & Schuster.

Knoblauch, C. H., and Lil Brannon. 1981. "Teacher Commentary on Student Writing: The State of the Art." *Freshman English News* 10 (2): 1–3.

Lessing, Doris. 1963. "A Woman on a Roof." In *A Man and Two Women,* 72–82. New York: Simon & Schuster.

Li, Xiao Ming. 1996. *"Good Writing" in Cross-Cultural Context.* Albany: SUNY Press.

Lowman, Joseph. 1995. *Mastering the Techniques of Teaching.* 2d ed. San Francisco: Jossey-Bass.

Macrorie, Ken. 1996. *Uptaught.* Portsmouth, NH: Boynton/Cook.

Market Data Retrieval. *College Faculty & Administrator Mailing Lists, 1997–98,* 46. Shelton, CT: Market Data Retrieval.

McLeod, Susan H. 1997. *Notes on the Heart: Affective Issues in the Writing Classroom.* Carbondale: Southern Illinois University Press.

McVay, Christina. 1998. E-mail to the author. 1 November.

Merrill, Robert. 1992. "Against the 'Statement.'" *College Composition and Communication* 43: 154–58.

Munter, Mary. 1996. *Guide to Managerial Communication.* 4th ed. Englewood Cliffs, NJ: Prentice-Hall.

Murray, Donald. 1997. *The Craft of Revision.* 3d ed. Fort Worth: Harcourt.

———. 1993. *Read to Learn.* 3d ed. Fort Worth: Harcourt.

———. 1985. *A Writer Teaches Writing.* 2d ed. Boston: Houghton Mifflin.

Murray, Frank B. 1996. "Beyond Natural Teaching: The Case for Professional Education." In *The Teacher Educator's Handbook,* edited by Frank B. Murray, 3–13. San Francisco: Jossey-Bass.

National Center for Educational Statistics. 1997. *The Condition of Education.* Washington: U.S. Department of Education.

———. "Indicator 41: Current Public Expenditure on Education as a Percentage of Total Public Expenditure: Private spending plays a role in education financing." Education Indicators: An International Perspective. 1996. 2 pp. Available <http://nces.ed.gov/pubs/eiip/eiip41s1.html>. 30 Sept. 1998.

Noddings, Nel. 1984. *Caring: A Feminine Approach to Ethics and Moral Education.* Berkeley: University of California Press.

Noguchi, Rei R. 1991. *Grammar and the Teaching of Writing.* Urbana, IL: NCTE.

O'Brien, Tim. 1990. *The Things They Carried.* New York: Penguin.

Rich, Adrienne. 1979. "Claiming an Education." In *On Lies, Secrets, and Silence,* 76–84. New York: W. W. Norton.

Rief, Linda. 1992. *Seeking Diversity.* Portsmouth, NH: Boynton/Cook.

Romano, Tom. 1995. *Writing with Passion.* Portsmouth, NH: Boynton/Cook.

———. 1987. *Clearing the Way.* Portsmouth, NH: Boynton/Cook.

Ronald, Ann. 1990. "Separate but (Sort of) Equal: Permanent Non-Tenure-Track Faculty Members in the Composition Program." *ADE Bulletin* 95: 33–37.

Sainte-Marie, Buffy. 1966. "My Country 'Tis of Thy People You're Dying." *Little Wheel Spin & Spin.* Vanguard.

Sanders, Scott Russell. 1986. "The Inheritance of Tools." *North American Review* (March): 55–58.

Spellmeyer, Kurt. 1989. "A Common Ground: The Essay in the Academy." *College English* 51 (3): 262–76.

Stanford, Gene, ed. 1979. *Classroom Practices in Teaching English, 1979-80: How to Handle the Paper Load.* Urbana, IL: NCTE.

Swift, Marvin. 1973. "Clear Writing Means Clear Thinking Means . . ." *Harvard Business Review* 51 (1): 59–62.

Timpson, William M., Suzanne Burgoyne, Christine S. Jones, and Waldo Jones. 1997. *Teaching and Performing: Ideas for Energizing Your Classes.* Madison: Magna.

Tobin, Lad. 1993. *Writing Relationships.* Portsmouth, NH: Boynton/Cook.

Wallace, M. Elizabeth. 1994. "Lower than the Low One on the Totem Pole: Teaching Writing to Oregon College Students." In *Paper Graders,* edited by Barry Roberts Greer, 16–35. Corvallis, OR: Cairn Press.

Weaver, Constance. 1996. *Teaching Grammar in Context.* Portsmouth, NH: Boynton/Cook.

Wells, Judy. 1991. *The Part-Time Teacher.* Willits, CA: Rainy Day Women Press. (Available through <jwells@stmarys-ca.edu>.)

White, E. B. 1966. "Once More to the Lake." In *One Man's Meat,* 215–21. New York: Harper.

Williams, Joseph. 1997. *Style—Ten Lessons in Clarity and Grace.* 5th ed. New York: Longman.

Wilson, Robin. 1998. "Universities Scramble to Find Teachers of Freshman Composition." *The Chronicle of Higher Education,* 3 October, A12–A14.

Index